PRAISE FOR *LEVELING UP*

"Great leaders ask great questions. In *Leveling Up*, Ryan provides 12 fundamental questions that will help you grow as a leader, advance in your influence, and make a difference in the world. *Leveling Up* is concise, powerful, and timely for any leader at any level."

—BRAD LOMENICK, FOUNDER OF BLINC AND AUTHOR
OF *H3 LEADERSHIP* AND *THE CATALYST LEADER*

"*Leveling Up* represents a tangible challenge to engage in internal dialog about what matters most in both your personal and professional life. As much as this book aims to inspire personal change, I found it to be a personal call to action through real and relevant questioning. The impact of Ryan's work is shown by the engagement of those around him. I feel that *Leveling Up* will leave a seismic wake for individuals, families, corporations, and the greater culture at large."

—ANDY BIRDSONG, ASSISTANT GENERAL
MANAGER, BROOKLYN NETS

"*Leveling Up* is an absolute must-read for anyone who wants to raise their game and take their personal development to the next level! We have used Ryan's twelve questions in our coaching work with athletes in the NFL, NBA, and with executives at Fortune 500 companies across the country. These pages are filled with incredible wisdom and practical applications for living into the best version of you. Ryan Leak is one of the most gifted communicators of our time. His thought-provoking words in *Leveling Up* will leave you inspired and excited to chase down your God-given giftedness!"

—JORDAN MONTGOMERY, SPEAKER AND
CEO OF MONTGOMERY COMPANIES

"People love to talk about 'leveling up' but I have never seen it spelled out masterfully like Ryan does! These twelve questions will absolutely change the game in your personal and professional life. It did for me! I keep coming back to them every week to review and sharpen! And the best thing about Ryan, he lives what he preaches. He is the real deal!"

—DAVID NURSE, NBA LIFE OPTIMIZATION COACH,
MOTIVATIONAL KEYNOTE SPEAKER, AND BESTSELLING AUTHOR

"The twelve questions posed in Ryan Leak's *Leveling Up* bring his executive coaching practice directly to the reader. Leaders at any level in pursuit of growth should be asking themselves these questions and discussing with their teams."

—CHRISTINE MEHRER, GROUP MANAGER,
MEETINGS, EVENTS, AND TRADESHOWS, BOSTON SCIENTIFIC

"Ryan has created the perfect playbook of simple, yet profound questions that stop us in our tracks to check ourselves and others along the leadership journey. As someone who develops and accelerates female leaders into executive-level positions, the twelve questions are critical in pumping the gas pedal."

—CAROL SEYMOUR, CEO OF SIGNATURE LEADERS AND AUTHOR
OF *WISDOM WARRIORS: JOURNEYS THROUGH LEADERSHIP AND LIFE*

"As a leader you will get to the point where you can provide unique opportunities for others. It won't be about giving someone a promotion or a project. It will be about building a ship and letting it go, so that other people will sail on without you. They might steer the ship differently than you, but even from the shore it will be the best ride in your life. Ryan's framework helps you understand why building that boat is so critical to leveling up your leadership by creating the dream sail for those that are ready for a new journey."

—PAT CONNELLY, HEAD OF STRATEGY AND
OPERATIONS, US ONCOLOGY, TAKEDA ONCOLOGY

"Communication is key to the success of any organization and the ability to steer our teams to be self-aware and true self leaders based on Ryan's fundamental structure, was an appropriate approach to remind them on how valuable their contribution is and how it influences our brand vision."

—Iris Diaz, Chief Marketing Officer,
Dallas Mavericks

"*Chasing Failure* was the book that sent me on a wild entrepreneurship journey. The pushing past my comfort zone to pursuing my dreams lead me to become recognized as one of the most notable people in travel by Travel + Leisure, run a successful content creation company, and now host my very own adventure travel show with Nat Geo—as a plus size black man you never see anyone that looks like me have a show of this caliber! *Leveling Up* is a book that I desperately needed personally and professionally in this new season I've walked in. *Leveling Up* is a must-read and just like *Chasing Failure*, Ryan Leak has brought us a new book that is life-changing!"

—Jeff Jenkins, Author at Chubby Diaries,
Award-Winning Content Creator and
Speaker, Adventure Travel Host

"How do you know if you are living as your highest and best self? How do you know if you are truly bringing your A game into all areas of your life? Ryan Leak's new book inspires you to do just that. You may be terrific in one area of your life but suboptimal in others. Through gentle challenges, guided wisdom, and plenty of inspiration, he leads you through a discovery and self-evaluation that will absolutely up your game and create magic in your life. Grab the book and make your life even better!"

—Hesha Abrams, Author of *Holding the Calm: The Secret to Resolving Conflict and Defusing Tensions*

"If you're a leader looking to challenge yourself and grow in self-awareness and impact, *Leveling Up* is a great read in helping you take your personal journey to new heights. Ryan asks twelve questions to help shed new light on your actions, your motivations, and the impact you have on others, and couples them with simple steps to help you build a bridge from who you are to who you want to be. As a corporate leader, husband, and father, you can get distracted by the demands of the moment and lose sight of the bigger picture and the real impact you can have on those around you. Ryan does a masterful job of asking the tough questions in challenging you to see yourself through the eyes of others, and to seek input from those who may see things you can't. As a leader, each day is an opportunity to grow. The book is insightful, thought-provoking, but also incredibly pragmatic in giving you a new lens on the choices we make every day and how simple changes can have a material impact. In *Leveling Up*, Ryan asks us to reflect on the legacy we want to leave, and then challenges us to live and move in a way that brings that closer to reality."

—GREG WILLIS, VICE PRESIDENT OF GLOBAL
SALES, LINKEDIN MARKETING SOLUTIONS

"There is no silver bullet in business or in life; the silver bullet is continuous improvement. So if you want to be successful, focus on getting a little bit better everyday. I can't think of a better book to help you do that than this one."

—TIM SCHURRER, AUTHOR OF *THE SECRET SOCIETY OF
SUCCESS* AND CEO OF DAVID NOVAK LEADERSHIP

LEVELING UP

12 QUESTIONS TO ELEVATE YOUR PERSONAL AND PROFESSIONAL DEVELOPMENT

RYAN LEAK

W PUBLISHING GROUP

AN IMPRINT OF THOMAS NELSON

Published in Nashville, Tennessee, by W Publishing, an imprint of Thomas Nelson.

Author is represented by the literary agency of The Fedd Agency, Inc., P. O. Box 341973, Austin, Texas, 78734.

Thomas Nelson titles may be purchased in bulk for educational, business, fundraising, or sales promotional use. For information, please email SpecialMarkets@ThomasNelson.com.

Any internet addresses, phone numbers, or company or product information printed in this book are offered as a resource and are not intended in any way to be or to imply an endorsement by Thomas Nelson, nor does Thomas Nelson vouch for the existence, content, or services of these sites, phone numbers, companies, or products beyond the life of this book.

ISBN 978-0-7852-6162-9 (HC)
ISBN 978-0-7852-4100-3 (eBook)
ISBN 978-0-7852-4101-0 (audiobook)
ISBN 978-0-7852-4099-0 (TP)

Library of Congress Control Number: 2022942192

Printed in the United States of America
23 24 25 26 27 LBC 5 4 3 2 1

To the life and memory of Ricky Texada.
You were a voice of wisdom during the most formidable
years of building my family and career. Thank you for
always making sure I kept my eyes on what matters most.
This book wouldn't be possible without your mentorship.

CONTENTS

CONTENTS

INTRODUCTION

I have a problem.

I have this habit of telling people I can do stuff I've never done. Like the one time my friend asked me if I could speak for their company.

I said, "Sure, no problem."

She responded, "Well, what about a full day of workshops? Could you lead our whole staff development day?"

Confidently, I said, "Of course."

Why? Why in the world would I tell her I could develop her whole staff of one hundred over the course of eight hours on a Monday when all I had ever done for anybody was deliver a sixty-minute keynote? I had no earthly idea how to pull it off, but I'm so glad I accepted the assignment.

I'll never forget it. I spent one of the eight hours in the workshop on kindness. Why? Because it's one of the few things you can't get a master's degree in that many companies desperately need. FYI, the company was a *bank*. I probably should have designed a day around leadership, customer service, and sales strategy for the twenty-first-century consumer. But for some odd reason, my friend green-lighted kindness hour. During that hour, people were tasked with going around and saying kind things to one another as I attempted to prove to this bank how kindness could change their entire business.

I kicked off the session by sharing a story with the bank about one of my favorite stores in the world. It is called the 99 Cents Only

Store. What I love about the 99 Cents Only Store is that it's one cent cheaper than dollar stores. Life is expensive, and I just like how the 99 Cents Only Store makes me feel. Don't judge me.

Once, I went there two days before Christmas. It was my goal to track down items that should not be ninety-nine cents. For instance, I found ankle braces that are normally forty dollars at Dick's Sporting Goods, and I asked the manager, "Are these ninety-nine cents?"

He replied, "Sir, yes, they are ninety-nine cents."

I've got two ankles, but I bought three. Why? Because for ninety-nine cents, why not?

I was so happy in this store that while I was in line, I told the cashier I would cover all of the items the person in front of me had at the time. She had five items. Do the math. We're at $4.95 plus tax. It's not that generous, but it was Christmas.

The woman turned around, looked at me, and said, "Is this a prank?"

I said, "Ma'am, do you think people are going around doing five-dollar pranks?"

She responded, "Are you serious?"

I said, "Ma'am, of course. It's Christmas." Then she told me something I absolutely didn't expect.

She said, "Sir, I have never had someone show me this much kindness in my whole life."

The point I made at that bank's staff development day was simple: we only have to be a little kind to make a big difference. People live in a pretty mean world. What if we can change it one act of kindness at a time?

At the end of that workshop, we did a question-and-answer session. A woman stood up and said, "Ryan, I don't have a question. I just want to say thank you. I grew up in a pretty volatile home. I went to a really competitive college. I just transitioned from another company where I learned that the only way to climb the ladder of success is to pull someone else off. I live in a dog-eat-dog world. But today, you taught me that I could actually get ahead in my career and in my life by being kind. I have never heard anything like that in my life. And if I'm honest, I don't like the person I've become. But today, you gave me a new way to be human. So no question for me. Just wanted to say thanks for coming."

That moment changed my life and career. I learned then that behind a coveted job title and salary was a woman just trying to figure out who she was. And I discovered there are so many more people just like her.

This realization is what led me to C-suite executive coaching. I wanted to have a career where I helped people win at work and win at home, even people who were crushing one aspect of their lives but struggling in others. Often we're expected to take our careers to the next level while also attempting to manage our love lives, raise children, show up for our friends, and remain healthy—mind, body, and soul.

For way too long, work and life have been in this tug-of-war battle in the conversation around work-life balance. It is almost as if we're being forced to pick between being good at work versus being good at life. However, contrary to popular belief, I think you can level up in your career and in your personal life at the same time.

For people who want the best of both worlds, some would say, "You can't have your cake and eat it too." But who buys a cake not to eat it? I think the biggest problem is, when trying to find balance, *work* always gets on the scale first before *life*.

Billions of dollars are spent every year training employees on how to be better at work. Higher education courses are primarily designed to prepare students for their future vocations. Conferences are crafted to help leaders develop strategies to grow their careers. But how many resources are collectively spent on taking areas outside of our careers to the next level? But I believe our careers will grow when we do. It's remarkable the number of successful people who have accomplished so many of their career goals but don't have five people in the world they can truly call their friends. They're crushing it at work. Yet, they're lonely in their personal lives.

Perhaps the only way to achieve work-life success is to consider putting some of our resources on the *life* side. In fact, if you level up in your personal life, it'll make leveling up in your professional career way easier. The reverse is not true. When you put all your eggs in leveling up in your professional career, it often comes at the expense of your personal life.

What I've learned from speaking at some of the top organizations in the world and working with C-suite executives, NBA athletes, and thousands of leaders is that the people who are consistently excelling in the most important areas of their lives have mastered the art of self-leadership. They have a set of principles set up that allow them to continue to grow. They understand that the growth and development of their lives and careers is their responsibility. They're not waiting for someone else to come challenge them. They've figured out ways to lead themselves when no one else is around.

When it comes to your growth and development, you might be tempted to believe it hinges on someone else to lead you well. But leveling up is *your* responsibility. It starts with *you*.

You are likely in one of two categories.

The first is you work for somebody. Most people do. Your leader could be phenomenal, adequate, mediocre, or terrible. A recent survey from job site Monster.com polled 957 people over one month who were openly seeking new jobs. The company asked why they wanted to leave their current employer. Seventy-six percent of them blamed a "toxic" boss for being the reason.[1] Many factors contribute to that, but the reality is I don't meet many people who say they have a phenomenal leader. If you do, you are part of a very small percentage. Let's call that the top 5 percent.

The remaining 95 percent of leaders fall in the terrible to adequate categories. It takes a lot to get in the phenom territory. So, depending on the category you'd put your leader in, the trajectory of your career could simply end up wherever they take it if you've put it in their hands.

And what exactly is your leader responsible for? Training you on company processes and procedures? Casting vision? Developing strategy? Okay, that's fine. But are they supposed to transform you into someone who works harder, brings a positive attitude, and owns the mistakes he or she makes? Are they supposed to make you a better friend, partner, spouse, or parent? A better person? That's a tall order, even for a phenomenal leader.

Now let's say you're in the second category, and *you're* the leader. You started the company. You were promoted. Your family owns the business. While there are perks to the position, what often doesn't come with the salary is a leader for you. When supply chain disruptions, labor shortages, and talent retention threaten your business, who's there to calm your fears? When others are asking you for vision for the future and you can't see it, who's there to give you advice? It's hard to go to the next level when you feel like no one is giving you the tools to get there. It can be lonely at the top, right?

Whether we're in charge or working for someone who is, many obstacles can keep us from leveling up in work and life, but make no mistake about it, our biggest hurdle is us! I love what motivational speaker Jim Rohn used to say: "If you don't like where you are, change it. You are not a tree."

That's why I wrote this book, so people could move up to the next level in their lives and careers. When it comes to the most important areas of your life and career, there are levels to it.

Level 1: Aimless

You have no earthly idea what you're doing or where you're going. You have no direction.

Level 2: Stuck

You can envision yourself doing better but can't seem to get out of a rut. You might work hard but experience very little progress.

Level 3: Coasting

You are going through the motions. Your life is on cruise control. You do what you have to do to survive.

Level 4: Developing

You are steadily growing. You've had incremental improvements over the past few years, and your relationships and career have excelled.

Level 5: Thriving

You are operating in your sweet spot. You don't *have* to do anything. You *get* to do everything.

Level 6: Mastery

You are doing so well that you're in a place to help others do the same.

Can you identify what level you are at in your life and career? You may have different answers for both. (We've developed a Leveling Up Assessment at ryanleak.com/levelingup to help you identify which level you are at now and to provide a few resources to get you where you want to be in the future.)

Most people I sit with live and work around level 2 and 3. They're stuck or coasting. They're in relationships and careers they tolerate. The goal of this book is to help you level up to a place where you feel like you're in such a sweet spot professionally and personally that you can help others get there too. As a speaker and coach, I'm often tempted to give people the answers they need to level up. But what I've learned in sessions with clients from my executive coaching practice is that there is a common thread and frequent statement they use: *That's a good question*. It's the questions I ask that perpetuate their growth beyond the counsel I may provide. When it comes to leveling up, questions are often better than answers because questions equip people to lead themselves when no one else is around.

In this book, I have designed twelve loaded questions that will help you go to the next level in your professional and personal life. These questions often lead you to other questions that ultimately will make you a better person and employee. These questions have been formed from countless coaching sessions, keynote experiences, and interviews.

This book's journey actually began with twenty-one questions. As companies requested me to speak, I would present all twenty-one questions and let them choose which ones they thought best spoke to their employees' pain points. At the end of the keynotes, I would poll the audience to learn which questions resonated with them the most and why. Sometimes, the company would even suggest a new question. Over time, twelve questions have risen to the top as those that help people level up the most.

Some of the questions involve you taking a hard look in the mirror, and you'll have to answer those for yourself. Then there are questions that involve you inviting a friend to the table to give you a fresh perspective. We need the mirror and the friend to level up. While the questions are best approached in order, you can dip in and out of the book. There might be a question that particularly speaks to you more than others. Feel free to begin there.

When it comes to the energy and focus you bring to your life and career, there are levels to it. Let these questions be your next-level guide when your career or life has plateaued, and you'll find yourself growing like never before.

CHAPTER 1

THE VISION QUESTION

What is my definition of success?

*Success is liking yourself, liking what you
do, and liking how you do it.*
—Maya Angelou

You want to know who's really good at bringing up your past? *Facebook.*

I always smile whenever I get a notification letting me know what I was up to five years ago. It is both nostalgic and laughable as I look at where I was, who I was with, and what I thought was fashionable. What's even more embarrassing is opening a school yearbook from the late 1990s when I was in grade school. It's mesmerizing to see what world I lived in and what I deemed successful and not successful.

I grew up in a lower-income neighborhood but had a scholarship that enabled me to go to a private school across town with people who had way more resources than my family did. Most of my neighbors worked blue-collar jobs in factories, while the parents of the kids where I went to school were in white-collar professions.

From an early age, I was operating in two different worlds, trying to figure out who I wanted to be and who I thought I had to be in order to be successful. Success for me meant you were good at sports, especially if you were tall. As a kid growing up playing basketball at the park on my side of town, my dream was to play in the NBA. But my friends from school, even the tall ones, wanted to be doctors, lawyers, astronauts, maybe even the president. I quickly discovered that the cars, homes, and restaurants on the other side of town were quite nicer than the ones in my own neighborhood.

If being a star athlete was my first idea of success, every decade I was handed a new one. As I went through grade school in the 1990s, success was showing up with the right school supplies. If you didn't have a Five Star Notebook, you were nobody. I came home from the first day of second grade and begged my mom to buy me one along with gel pens. I was sure that a Five Star Notebook held the key to everything I needed to be successful.

Or the real holy grail: Beanie Babies. Recently, a Steg the Stegosaurus, the coveted mottled brown dinosaur, sold for $40,000 on eBay.[1] Little did I know, had I owned it as a child, I would have been considered cool back then and $40,000 richer right now!

In the 2000s, success was determined by cell phones. Not just the phones themselves—although a BlackBerry or a blinged-out Sidekick was the gold standard—but the actual phone plans had levels. Just because you *had* a cell phone didn't mean you could make calls anytime like we do today. Your minutes were limited, and how many you had and when you could use them depended on your cell plan with your cell phone provider. Even your texts were capped. You might have had to convince your parents that adding texting to the family plan was worth the investment.

If you had AT&T, for example, your friends could call you after 7:00 p.m. and be set; however, your buddy with Verizon wouldn't have free minutes until 9:00 p.m. There was a lot of work involved in figuring out when others could talk. Of course, the worst was running out of minutes and having to resort to using the home phone. But true success was when someone had unlimited minutes and could be on the phone all day, every day.

Thankfully, my ideas about success have continued to evolve as I've gotten older. I can still wake up every now and then thinking success for me equates to a specific car, social media influence, bestseller lists, or speaking at megachurches and Fortune 500 companies. But what I've figured out about success is that you have to have your own definition of it in order to avoid living out someone else's.

My job is not to tell you what success should look like for you. My goal in this chapter is to help you unpack the question, What is *my* definition of success? Your answer should be both authentic to you and clearly articulated, because at the end of the day, your goals need to align with *your* definition of success and no one else's.

The first step isn't trying to define success for yourself right away. Instead, you have to put your existing ideas about success on the table and ask yourself where those ideas came from.

A '97 CHRYSLER TOWN & COUNTRY

I remember the first playdate I had with one of the kids from private school. A "playdate." That got my attention. In my neighborhood, we didn't have playdates. You just went outside with no real plan as to how that would transpire. Before our playdate, my friend's mom called my parents and asked, "We're going to come pick up Ryan and take him to lunch. How does 10:00 a.m. on Saturday sound?"

By 9:30 a.m. that Saturday, I was fully dressed, ready to go, and waiting at the window. I knew that if I could just make it to their side of town, my life would be amazing.

But what I was most excited for wasn't even going to lunch—it was the luxury vehicle they would be chauffeuring me in all day. I had seen their car, and, in my mind, it was 150 times nicer than ours. A sleek Chrysler with wood paneling on the side and a VCR in the back seat. It was *amazing*. I daydreamed about getting to ride in that car all over town, having my friends see me, and getting to experience that luxury and sophistication.

The vehicle I'd pinned all my dreams on that day was a '97 Chrysler Town & Country. I even envied friends who had conversion vans. Conversion vans were like mini hotels on wheels. They had blinds, a small bed, and an entertainment system in the back. Back then, I thought this vehicle was the pinnacle of wealth.

But all the things I desperately wanted as a kid—a wood-paneled Chrysler, a conversion van, gel pens, Beanie Babies, Pokémon cards, more night and weekend minutes for my phone, unlimited texting—seem ridiculous now. Back then, I thought having all that would make my life great. Yet the things I once thought of as being a matter of life or death, I wouldn't even want now.

I'm confident the stuff I wanted twenty years ago wouldn't make me feel successful today, but I wonder if I haven't just come up with a list of replacement items. Has that burning desire for a Chrysler minivan just been replaced with my hopes for the newest and fastest electric car on the market? Have unlimited minutes and text messages been replaced with frequent flier miles and travel reward points?

Unless we do a lot of work to unpack why we want the things we want—whether that's a car, a house, a job, a following, or any other achievement—it may be impossible to know. I have a suspicion that what we *want* is often flawed by what we *wanted*. What we wanted in the past forces us to question what we so desperately want in the present.

I didn't start to question my definition of success until I began seeing "successful" people die by suicide or drug overdose. I also had a front-row seat to seeing some of the wealthiest people I knew get divorced, split their families, and lose their most treasured relationships. Suddenly, success for them moved from having the ability to own a second home to simply having their kids visit them at any home for holidays.

We all got our ideas about success from somewhere. Most started at home, but we are also products of our greater environments.

Whether it's our neighborhood, the region or the country we live in, our socioeconomic class, our religion, our race, our gender, or the generation in which we are born, a lot goes into influencing what we think we want. None of us are born and raised in a vacuum. We are constantly bombarded with messages telling us what we should want and aspire to be.

In my estimation, here in the United States, success used to be measured by fame and fortune. I was doing some reading about Baby Boomers, and the author suggested that the way that generation showed they had money was by how nice their stuff was. Think about the American dream with its 2.5 kids and a beautiful house with a big green lawn surrounded by a white picket fence. For an entire generation, that was considered making it.

Before social media, if I achieved my definition of success, nobody knew. My neighbors, classmates, and friends only knew I was making it if they came over and witnessed it. Maybe people who had really done something ended up in the newspaper, but the events of our lives, both the highs and lows, were only shared if people personally knew us. But then came social media, and a new category of success was created. Shares. Likes. Pokes. Retweets. Quote tweets. Views. Comments. Replies. Followers. Subscribers. Downloads.

Back when Facebook was so exclusive that the only way you could get an account was to go to a big-name college, I remember being offered a job. When I asked what made them pick me, the guy said, "Man, you have two thousand friends on Facebook. I don't know anybody who has two thousand friends on Facebook."

No one would hire me based on my Facebook friends now

because it doesn't matter, but the truth is, it didn't matter then either. Not when it came to my ability to do that job well. But that's what got this hiring manager's attention. He thought it made me special.

The power of social media attention is now so great that I believe people would be influencers without pay just to say they were. This despite the fact that some of the highest-profile influencers have quit the platform. They had some people's "dream jobs," but they were too depressed, anxious, and burned out to stay. And those who have stayed have begun to speak out about the mental health issues they are dealing with as a result of their success.[2]

One TikToker, a guy named Sha Crow, with over 550,000 followers, recorded a video that went viral explaining how many mental health issues he and his influencer friends now deal with as a result of their success. The comments section was filled with even more influential influencers agreeing with him. "Mood," wrote one guy with five million followers, roughly the population of Minnesota.

I hear Sha Crow, but don't we all want to be admired? Don't we want people to think highly of us? Don't we all want to be liked? If we're really honest, I think we all want to be *adored*. Or dare I say, idolized? It's called *American Idol* for a reason. We have to be careful not to be so consumed with *looking* successful that we miss out on actually *being* successful. You can look rich and be broke. You can take a beautiful family photo and hate the people in the picture.

SUCCESS IN THEIR EYES

To find true success is to understand where your current definition of success comes from and make it yours. We've already talked about how your upbringing and the cultural environment in which you live can hugely impact your metric for success, but many other factors about you could lead you to strive for someone else's standard.

For some men, the metric for success is to look like Dwayne Johnson, perform like Tony Robbins, and be able to spend like Elon Musk. For some women, the metric for success is equally unrealistic, especially for working mothers. They are expected not only to look good, perform well, and make a decent living, but also to raise amazing little humans.

One study following gifted people over four decades of their high-performance careers found that both male and female participants agreed that family was their best accomplishment, but men valued their ability to support their families financially, while women valued having given their families their emotional energy and time.[3] All other factors being constant, their definition of success was informed by their gender.

For the academic world, success becomes all about GPA, multiple degrees, tenure, or publications. For social media, it's all about going viral and having high engagement. For churches, success is often determined by how many people show up on a weekend. In politics, it is funding *and* votes. In professional sports, it is championship rings and public perception. In music, it is Grammys. In film, it is Oscars. In law firms, it is making partner. At networking events, success is defined by who you know.

Pick your industry, and you will find a metric that was handed to you. You may attain success in one of those arenas, but can you really say it was done by *your* definition of success?

Whether it's grades or a piece of jewelry or a job title, we all have ideas about what it means to be a successful person. Early on, we were told it was driving a certain car, having a certain degree—and that image stuck. If I asked you to picture someone successful, what would that person look like to you? For many, that person would be rich, well-dressed, wearing a nice watch and cool sneakers, hopping on a private jet for a private island vacation, all while being filmed.

Go to any event and whoever is sitting courtside or backstage, we think they must be successful. On a flight, you'll likely walk past people sitting in first class and you'll think, "They *must* be successful." (Unless you're on Southwest. And then it's the Group A people who are VIP.)

We might not be successful, but if we fly first class, we *feel* successful. Anything we believe the average person can't experience becomes desirable to us. It allows us to look at our yardstick and decide we made it. We are better. We are elite. Even if the gap between our advertised success and our actual success is huge, we think, *As long as I'm doing slightly better than them, I'm successful.*

Comparison is a dangerous game—and it works in reverse. Maybe you're making $400,000 a year, but your friends all founded tech startups worth millions, so now you feel poor. The image of success we have when we are young, and consistently build on, is usually construed in relation to others' successes or failures.

What we all need to do is put down our phones, look away from the internet, and pause long enough to ask ourselves: Is the definition we have of success ours?

Because if you are not careful, someone else is going to set the bar for you.

You can't know for sure whether you are following your own North Star unless you are able to move from an *external* definition of success to an *internal* one. We each must define success for ourselves, and we start by unpacking where our ideas about success came from. Otherwise, we risk being steered in directions we shouldn't go.

But knowing where your ideas of success came from is only

half your assignment. Once you know that—and recognize who is influencing you—you also need to develop clarity of vision around your goals.

DEFINE YOUR TOUCHDOWNS

I am not here to guilt anyone for their definition of success. I simply want you to be able to define in clear terms what you want from your life.

On the professional side, that could be your income, career trajectory, revenue, sales numbers, or employee count. On the personal side, success actually *can* be a car, a house, a certain neighborhood, or a degree. Whatever it is, you need to be able to identify it.

What is your own internal definition of success?

When I ask this question in professional settings, most people hesitate to say money. But the reality is, if it is money, they just need to be honest with themselves about that. So, let's say your definition of success is money, then you need to answer this: What amount of money would make you feel successful? What number would be enough? Most people's number is "more," which is why they never feel successful. But if you have a number, write it down. It's your touchdown.

If your goal is headcount in your business, that also must be a clear number. If your definition of success is a "what"—if it can successfully fill in the blank in the sentence, "If I have _____, then I will be successful"—you need to have specific details about your *what*. If it's a car, what car? If it's a home, what kind, what size, and what part of town? If it's being able to afford a pair of exclusive sneakers, which ones?

The trouble with not having a clear definition of what a touchdown and win is for you, for your family, or for your team, is if you hit it, you won't know when to celebrate. And because you won't know when and what to celebrate, your life will become a place where you just move around, never taking a moment to feel your success and smell the roses.

A study of lottery winners found that winning the lottery, the literal metaphor we use for the best thing that can happen to us, didn't make them happier. Instead, the winners adapted to their new circumstances, and the bar was raised.[4] That dissatisfaction chases all of us, especially if we haven't been analytical about where our goals came from. Your small business might be having a runaway year, but it's not public. Or your business went public, but the stock price didn't do what you wanted it to. Or the IPO went well, but now you have switched your focus to worrying about reporting quarterly earnings.

The trouble with poorly defined, external yardsticks is that there will always be someone richer, more famous, more followed, or more applauded to compare yourself to. Again, whatever your yardstick for success is, you need to own that. But I would argue that success is more nuanced than a *what*. What if success wasn't just what you achieved or what you got or what you wanted, but *who* you were becoming?

THANKSGIVING REGRETS

The problem with shifting the definition of success from a *what* to a *who* is that there aren't the same rewards, at least from our broader culture. When you get first place, you get a trophy. When you perform at work, you get a bonus. When you're the number one vlogger on YouTube, you get a lot of views, and you get paid. But when you are kind and generous to the people in your life, no one is going to hand you a medal.

The struggle to be a good person in a "What's in it for me?" society is real. No one is typically going to pay you for doing the right thing or being a thoughtful friend and neighbor.

What is unfortunate is that many studies have shown that generosity, or the ability to give to others, has a direct link to our own feelings of happiness. For example, one study looked at participants who were given one hundred dollars to spend over the course of a few weeks. Half the subjects were told to spend the money on themselves, the other half on other people. Guess who reported the greatest satisfaction afterward?[5] It was the subjects who spent the money on other people.

In my line of work, I spend a lot of time on stages. Whether I am delivering a message at a church or speaking in a corporate setting, when I do well, people take notice. I get attention, applause, views, likes—all of it. But no one sees when I am down on the ground pretending to be a dinosaur with my kids. No one sees me having an in-depth conversation with my wife. No one sees me showing up for a friend.

I don't do these things because I'm a good person. I do them because I have seen too many people achieve all of their professional goals while ignoring their personal goals. I will never be the anti-money guy, but I also believe our definition of success needs to be more holistic, even just for our own sakes. The time you spend on yourself might make you better, but the time you spend on others is a long-term investment in all your collective happiness.

It is worth asking yourself:

What can I do now to make sure that the people in my life actually want to be in it? What can I do now to make sure that my kids want to come home for Thanksgiving in the future?

What can I do now to make sure people want to work for me or with me long-term?

Will accomplishing all my professional hopes and dreams be

enough if the people I love most aren't on speaking terms with me because of what my professional goals required?

Right now, my kids are young. I know I will get to see them for the holidays. I know I have time to do things right and make things right when I get it wrong, but their presence isn't a guarantee forever. The reality is, we are all one empty Thanksgiving table away from wishing we had done it differently.

ENDGAME

One of the exercises we take clients through in our executive coaching practice is the Personal Vision Exercise.

It starts with answering this question: What's a word or two that *others* would use to describe you? Think about that for a second. You can ask someone to know for sure, or you can offer your own hypothesis. The second part of the exercise involves answering this: What's a word or two *you* would use to describe yourself?

I began this exercise with a client once and was curious what words others would use to describe her.

"Blunt and direct," she told me.

"Cool," I said. "Now choose one word to describe yourself."

"Fun!" she immediately answered.

Houston, we have a problem.

There's nothing wrong with being blunt or direct. But it's pretty far from fun. The only issue we have with being blunt or direct is nobody intentionally becomes that way. There's not an eighth grader in the world right now who is sitting around thinking, "One day, when I grow up, I want to be . . . blunt." But any one of us can accidentally end up blunt or direct. Sometimes life experiences can make us believe we have to be a certain way to survive. However, you're not going to take your life or career to the next level on accident. You have to be intentional.

That's why the crux of the exercise is answering a third question: What's one or two words *you want* others to use to describe you?

Most people don't know that they can choose their own word and strive for it. Most people believe they are a product of their environments. Some people may be naturally optimistic or pessimistic. Some people are naturally introverted or extroverted. But the best part of leveling up is that you get to choose what kind of person you want to be. Pick your word.

Brave
Diligent
Friendly
Joyful
Open-minded
Compassionate
Unique
Calming
Loyal
Authentic
Kind

You can actually *choose* the direction of your life. Sometimes one word can give you the vision you need to strive for. If you want to be described in a certain way, just make sure it's a true story. If you want others to say you're the most encouraging person they've ever worked with, start encouraging them. Nobody should have to lie about you to tell a good story.

Maybe your new definition of success is internal. Maybe you want to close the gap between the one word you have chosen for yourself and the one you would want to be described as. Maybe your new definition of success isn't a dollar amount but the impact you make on someone else's life.

Who we decide to be and the choices that result ultimately become something I think about a lot: legacy. Your legacy is your endgame. It is thinking about success through the lens of how your life will impact other people. That's how I landed on my word. How I want to be described by others is *generous*. That is why in my company and my home, we don't have revenue or income goals. We work and live by giving goals.

Every year, we set a goal for an amount we want to give away. That goal is the very thing that has taken our company to the next level. It is a personal value and a company value. How we measure and define success for us is how much we can support organizations and people trying to make a difference in the world. It is also how we leave the legacies we want to have at the end of our lives. We're driven by impact and generosity, which allows us to make that happen.

What drives you? How are you measuring your success? It can be measured by what you want to accomplish, and it can be measured by who you're becoming. I encourage you to do the Personal Vision Exercise and consider what you want the direction of your life and career to be marked by.

CHAPTER RECAP

- Our definition of success is often flawed by our past desires.
- Our definition of success isn't always our own but has been shaped by external influences, like our gender, race, nationality, or chosen industry.
- We need to create an internal definition of success with clearly defined goals.

- We have to be careful that our goals don't come at the cost of our personal life and relationships.

One way to ensure we have a holistic, thoughtful definition of success is to move from success being a *what* to a *who* we are becoming.

DO THIS NOW

The Personal Vision Exercise
Ask yourself:

1. What's a word or two that *others* would use to describe me?
2. What's a word or two *I* would use to describe myself?
3. What's one or two words I want others to use to describe me?

CHAPTER 2

THE SELF-AWARENESS QUESTION

What is it like to be on the other side of me?

To know yourself, you must sacrifice the illusion that you already do.
—Vironika Tugaleva

Have you ever met someone who thought they were a good singer but couldn't carry a note to save their life? In their minds, they sound like Adele or John Legend. In everyone else's minds, they belong on the blooper reels for *The Voice*. Somewhere on their journey their mom lied to them, and they just kept going with it.

Have you ever worked with someone who simply wasn't self-aware? They'd hit Reply All on emails at all the wrong times. They had a habit of extending the length of meetings by rambling about things that added zero value to the team or project. They lacked the emotional intelligence to read a room or read a Zoom. They had a reputation for being rude but saw themselves as kind. They were extremely insecure but believed they came across as confident. They were given a position of leadership, but people only followed them because they didn't have a choice.

Are you related to someone who isn't self-aware? Perhaps it's an in-law who believes everyone loves their cooking. Or a cousin who can't see how their comments come across as passive-aggressive. Maybe you have a sibling who doesn't realize everyone has grown weary of their sarcasm.

All these people have no clue what it is like to be on the other side of them. But, have you ever considered that *you* could be this person?

What typically happens whenever self-awareness is brought up is that we immediately think of someone else who needs it. We all *think* we are self-aware, and we all believe others aren't. The irony of self-awareness is that you would have to be *extremely* self-aware to know that you're *not* self-aware. How many times have you heard someone admit they're not self-aware? Not many, if ever, right? Self-awareness is the biggest problem none of us believe we have.

In my executive coaching practice, I've found that the people who believe they're the most self-aware are actually the least. When I'm working with a company, I'm there to help solve problems. What often happens when I'm doing a discovery call is that most of the problems that are shared aren't problems, they're *people*. They're not *what* problems. They're *who* problems. Someone on the call believes a specific person in the organization is the problem. But the bigger problem with the person they believe is the problem . . . is that person . . . believes *somebody else* is the problem. And on and on.

When I ask leaders where their biggest challenges or weaknesses are, they point at their teams. However, when I ask teams what needs to be better, they almost always cite problems in leadership. When I ask each group what the other's contributions are, the answers almost never match. There is a profound incongruence between what most people believe it's like to be on the other side of them and what it's *actually* like.

Have you considered what it's like to be on the other side of you in your personal and professional life? Not what you want people to think or the narratives you have created about yourself, but how people experience you in real time?

Answering this question can be difficult. Instead, ask yourself:

- What is it like to be on the other side of my emails?
- What is it like to be on the other side of my parenting?
- What is like to be on the other side of my texts?
- What is it like to be on the other side of my Facebook comments?
- What is it like to be on the other side of my marriage?
- What is it like to be related to me?
- What is it like to be in meetings with me?
- What is it like to work with me?
- What is it like to work for me?
- What is it like to follow me?
- What is it like to be on the sidelines of my kid's game with me?
- What is it like to be coached by me?
- What is it like to be on a team with me?
- What is it like to travel with me?
- What is it like to do holidays with me?
- What is it like to be on a date with me?
- What is it like to live next to me?
- What is it like to live with me?
- What is it like to be my friend?

You may be thinking that being on other side of you is remarkable. But are you sure?! A word of practical advice as you sit with these questions (and whatever other ones they inspire): assume you're not self-aware, and err on the side of caution. Regardless of your season of life, all of us have room for improvement when it comes to self-awareness. Assume you move through the world with very little awareness of how you impact the people around you.

I approach self-awareness as a lifestyle, much like how we

approach being healthy. You never get to a place where you've eaten enough vegetables that you can take a year off. Self-awareness is a journey I believe we all should be on and remain on.

This advice isn't meant to generate negative self-talk for you. Instead, use this as an opportunity to step back and then step into someone else's shoes on the other side of you. Open your mind to the possibilities of what it might be like to experience you outside of your perspective. The more you are willing to become aware of that experience and the blind spots that we all unknowingly have, the more this chapter will help you level up.

BIOMYTHOGRAPHY

Recently, I have been captivated by the idea of *biomythography*. This is a literary term, "a style of composition that weaves myth, history, and biography in epic narrative."[1] It's basically the idea that you and I are consistently telling ourselves a story about ourselves and others that is intertwined with some truths and some myths.

It's easy to get wrapped into biomythography every day. We sit in the director's chair of our minds and tell a story that suits us best. Whenever there's any sort of conflict with someone in our personal or professional lives, our biggest temptation is to tell ourselves a story that makes *them* the villain and makes *us* the hero. The truth is, they're not that evil, and we don't wear capes and save people falling from skyscrapers.

It's easy to go to work and think we can do somebody else's job better than they can. It's easy to critique a leader from the sidelines. It's easy to think your marriage would be better if your spouse contributed more. It's easy to think your dating relationship would be better if your significant other was better at communicating. It's easy to believe that, in our stories, we're the ones putting up with everyone else's petty nonsense.

But have you ever stopped to think about how convenient a story that is for us to tell ourselves? Because those stories assume what? They assume we are amazing! Those stories assume that what it's like to be on the other side of us is utter euphoria. But is it?

The reality is, the stories we tell ourselves about other people are extremely flawed. And I'm willing to bet you'd say the stories other people tell themselves about you are extremely flawed. We know both of those to be true because none of us ever posts our truest story.

Your current profile picture and headshot is not an indication of who you are or what your life looks like. How often are you standing flawlessly in front of a white background where you get to tell a photographer to get your good side? How often are you on vacation smiling on the beach? We could look at one another's filtered and photoshopped pictures of our vacations and walk away with the story that our lives are pretty amazing when that could be the furthest thing from the truth.

It's paramount that we dismantle our biomythography to make sure we're not glorifying ourselves and demonizing others. Otherwise we become experts on what everyone else needs to do. We think the world would be a better place if other people would just get their acts together.

I wish I had a dollar for every time I've heard the phrase, "If they would just _____." That "they" can be any number of people. That externalized wish to change people becomes a formula that we apply broadly. "My life would be better if they would just . . ."

If my spouse would just . . .
If my partner would just . . .
If my kid would just . . .

If my friends would just . . .
If my boss would just . . .
If leadership would just . . .
If my employees would just . . .
If Democrats would just . . .
If Republicans would just . . .
If the president would just . . .
If men would just . . .
If women would just . . .
If Black people would just . . .
If white people would just . . .
If immigrants would just . . .

The truth is, the world would be a better place if *we* would just _____.

Unfortunately, you can't control what questions other people should be asking. You only have control over your own growth. Wishing someone else would do the same is no way to go to the next level. One of the biggest myths about growing in your life and career is believing that it'll happen when somebody else changes. You will grow when *you* change.

Consider how all the stories you tell about yourself place you in the center of the epic. Making the world a better place. Fighting injustice. Enduring everyone else's shortcomings. What I have learned from working with hundreds of organizations is that we are all keenly aware of what everyone else needs to work on. The problem with having those stories, with knowing everyone's faults but our own, is that we exist in other people's stories too. In those stories, we might not be the hero—in fact, it's very unlikely.

I can't promise that if you grow in self-awareness, you will be able to control what other people think of you. That is a futile dream. But the more you are aware of your impact on others, the better chance you have of not being someone else's nemesis—and the better chance you have of closing the gap between how you want to be described and how other people describe you.

Whose stories are you a character in? In what role do you wish to be cast? What do you think it's like for them when you play that role?

SELF-AWARE EXPERTS

Because self-awareness is so rare, it is important to spend some time describing what it means to be self-aware. The basic dictionary definition is: "an awareness of one's own personality or individuality."[2] I would argue this is incomplete, but it does point to an important element of cultivating self-awareness. This is a process that starts internally before becoming external.

Organizational psychologist Tasha Eurich, in her bestselling book *Insight*, examines the connection between self-awareness and success in the workplace. In a survey of studies on the topic, she found that self-awareness really has two components. The first is *internal self-awareness*, or "how clearly we see our own values, passions, aspirations, fit with our environment, reactions (including thoughts, feelings, behaviors, strengths, and weaknesses), and impact on others."[3]

"Know thyself" is an ancient Greek maxim that predates modern history by three hundred years.[4] In our quest to understand our impact on others, we first must be able to honestly look at ourselves. Self-aware people can articulate how they are feeling, what they think, and what they want.

The second type of self-awareness is *external self-awareness*, or "understanding how other people view us, in terms of" all the things we know about ourselves.[5] The science here is important.

Leaders who are good at assessing how their employees feel about them have better relationships with those employees because they see them as being empathetic and effective. The same could also be said of spouses and parents.

Interestingly, these two categories of self-awareness are not directly correlated. You might be excellent at examining your own impulses but have no idea how that translates to the outside world. Or you might be a keen observer of how you impact people without being grounded in your own true north (otherwise known as being a people pleaser).

The people who kill it at self-awareness can do both. These people are rare, and they are a pleasure to be around. They are effective in relationships. They are especially effective as leaders. They know how to listen to their teams, but they can create a vision and set the course. They are amazing as team members. They understand their role and are pumped to contribute. They are also incredible friends because they are aware when they've dominated the conversation. They can pivot to make space for you.

People gain this knowledge in different ways. Some people take StrengthsFinder tests or personality assessments. Other people have their ten thousand hours of experience and expertise. Still others have external validation from others who know what they are doing. But the mark of being great is never declaring that you are. If you declare yourself a great leader, you are probably not. If you say you are pretty self-aware, that is typically the first sign of someone who is not.

To put it simply, self-aware people do three things well:

1. They are aware of their strengths.
2. They are aware of their shortcomings.
3. They are aware of their impact on other people.

Are you aware of what you're good at, where you can improve, and how you make other people feel when you walk in the room? Being self-aware doesn't mean you are a perfect person. I know this feeling very well. Of the self-aware leaders I have worked with or met, they all have faults. Many of them work hard to create structure so that those weaknesses don't negatively impact the people around them. For example, I know several executives who are terrible with names. They have their assistants print out flashcards with people's pictures and names and spend hours studying them. They know what they aren't good at, but they want to improve.

Some people are good at email, quick to respond with informative but concise answers. Other people aren't. They take a full five days and then write long, rambling responses. These people might have an assistant help them filter their inbox, or maybe use a service like Grammarly (not an ad—although hit me up, Grammarly, I love your service) to make recommendations about word choice, sentence length, or tone. Being self-aware doesn't totally prevent you from making mistakes, but it might prevent those mistakes from becoming serious issues.

It is true that there are self-aware people who never take that next step. They know who they are, they know how they impact people, they know what people think of them . . . and they just don't care. If you don't care, it's going to be nearly impossible to go to the next level in any area of your life, especially at home.

Even if you don't care about leveling up, you still need to reckon with what it is like to be on the other side of you. If you are a jerk and that's your brand, it might work for a while, but eventually, people are going to fall away. People will choose to make less to not have to be around you. Some people will leave your life or divorce you to escape being around you. You don't want to get there before you start considering what it's like to be on the other side of you. You have the choice to be what and who you need to be, but be prepared to own the consequences.

TWO STEPS TO SELF-AWARENESS

If you have made it this far in this chapter, you have already begun the journey to self-awareness. Self-awareness starts by considering, from many angles and viewpoints, what it is like to be on the other side of you.

The more humility and openness you use to approach this question the better. Too many people assume they're awesome—it's awesome to be my friend, my husband, my child—when, like I said, you can do a lot more work by operating under the assumption that it also could be terrible.

Step #1: Ask the Mirror

The first step toward self-awareness is to ask the mirror. Take off the cape and honestly answer this question: What is it like to be on the other side of you in all aspects of your life? Run through the list of questions at the beginning of this chapter (page 18). Quiet down the voices that want to argue or prop up the myths you have about yourself.

The other day I was in my kitchen doing some work on my computer. My eight-year-old son was hanging around while I worked, interrupting every once in a while to ask a question. Every time he asked, I would answer him. Internally, I was frustrated (I wanted to be able to focus), but I didn't say anything I regretted.

After about five minutes of my short answers, he said, "Hey, Dad, I'm going to go sit on the couch so you can work."

"Why do you say that?" I asked.

He is too young to articulate how I was making him feel in that moment, but I didn't need him to say it out loud to get it. *Ryan, your body language says it all*, I thought. What was it like to be on the other side of me right then? Not fun. The gap between trying to be engaged and being engaged is monumental for an eight-year-old.

If you are always considering what it's like to be on the other side of you, it will change how you show up in the rest of your life. How you walk into the office. How you walk through your front door. This leads to paying more attention to how people respond to you. Whereas before you might have been caught up in the narrative in your head, now you are looking for signs of your impact.

Our words and actions, even our body language, scream out messages about us all the time. It might just be a brief interaction with someone, and he or she will have formed an impression of who you are and how you move in the world.

Step #2: Ask Someone Else

The internal monitoring of your impact on people is never done. You must stay vigilant and constantly sharpen your ability to be perceptive. That being said, your ability to self-diagnose your impact is going to be limited.

Data supports this. "Research has shown that we simply do not have access to many of the unconscious thoughts, feelings, and motives we're searching for," says Dr. Eurich.[6] When we try to be introspective and answer the "why" behind our motivations, behaviors, and beliefs, we usually fall short. We latch on to what *feels* true and invent reasons why it must be. We are unreliable narrators of our lives.

For self-awareness to really blossom, you must do something difficult: go ask people what they think of you. Answering the question, "What is it like to be on the other side of me?" requires other people. And it requires those people to be honest. You need an honest colleague, an honest family member, or an honest friend. To pull off self-awareness, you need an honest person who has a front-row seat to your life and is willing to give you real feedback. This is a very hard thing to do.

In his book *7 Simple Choices for a Better Tomorrow*, Bob Merritt has a chapter titled "Everybody Needs a Fred." Bob Merritt was the pastor of a very large church in Minnesota. The church had three hundred people in weekly attendance when he started as the pastor and over twenty-eight thousand people when he retired.

At one point in Bob's career, the church board was put in a position to address some leadership concerns around anger and abrasive language that were brought to their attention. They met without him to discuss whether or not he would be allowed to continue to lead the church. They voted to allow him to remain in his position if he agreed to enter into a full year of counseling with a guy named Fred.

Bob describes his process with Fred as painful and humiliating. Fred interviewed as many people as he possibly could who knew Bob, from people who worked for him to friends to family members. Fred asked all those people two questions:

What's good about Bob?
What's bad about Bob?

And they unloaded. When they met to discuss Fred's findings, to Bob's surprise, he was handed a 225-page document of feedback in detail about what the people in his life, professionally and personally, had said about him. They said things like . . .

Bob doesn't listen well.
Bob is unapproachable.
Bob speaks before he thinks.
I know Bob cares, but he's not gifted at showing it.

Bob read 225 pages of how people thought he was abrasive and unloving. For the first time in his life, he was confronted with what it was *really* like to be on the other side of him.

The one that hurt the most was from his son, fifteen at the time, who wrote: *My dad is angry a lot.* There was something about hearing that from his son that wrecked him—and there was something about hearing those words from his son that saved him.

Bob is a friend and mentor, and I've learned a lot from him. When he shares his story publicly, he says that his process with Fred saved his career, his marriage, and his life. I think Bob is right. Everybody needs a Fred. But my hope for you is that you won't need a 225-page wake-up call to start discovering what it's actually like to be on the other side of you.

ENDGAME TAKE TWO

Self-awareness ultimately ties back into your endgame. What do you want your impact to be? Knowing how you impact other people is fundamental to being able to successfully execute on your answer to that question.

We can continue to externalize that outward-facing empathy to people beyond our family, friends, and coworkers as well. This is an exercise you can do with people you hang with, live with, or work with.

What's it like to be on the other side of you? Inspiring? Encouraging? Difficult? Exhausting? When people experience you in life and work, what is their takeaway? Be considerate of how your words and actions impact other people. You may think you're pretty self-aware and you know what it's like to interact with you, but inviting someone else to weigh in is still a good idea. It will either reaffirm what you already think or give you a new perspective.

CHAPTER RECAP

- Most of us lack self-awareness. The more certain you are that you are self-aware, the more likely it is you aren't.
- We create narratives around our own lives, casting us as the heroes and others as villains. Be mindful of the story you are telling yourself.
- True self-awareness has two components: the internal (knowing our strengths and shortcomings) and external (knowing how we impact others).
- We need to invite someone in to verify what we think it's like to be on the other side of us.

DO THIS NOW

The Self-Awareness Inventory Exercise

1. Write down what you think it's like to be around you at home.
2. Write down what you think it's like to be around you at work.

CHAPTER 3

THE SELF-IMPROVEMENT
QUESTION

How can I get better?

*If you don't make the time to work on creating the life
you want, you're eventually going to be forced to spend
a lot of time dealing with a life you don't want.*
—Kevin Ngo

Michael Jordan is described on the official NBA website as:
"Rookie of the Year; Five-time NBA MVP; Six-time NBA
champion; Six-time NBA Finals MVP; Ten-time All-NBA First
Team; Nine-time NBA All-Defensive First Team; Defensive Player
of the Year; Fourteen-time NBA All-Star; Three-time NBA All-Star
MVP; 50th Anniversary All-Time Team; Retired with the NBA's
highest scoring average of 30.1 ppg; Hall of Fame inductee."[1]

And this is what they call a "brief" list of his accomplishments.

Jordan is considered by many to be basketball's GOAT—the
greatest of all time—but he wasn't even trying to be the best.
In an interview with Tony Robbins, Jordan said, "Every day I
demand more from myself than anybody else could humanly
expect. I'm not competing with somebody else. I'm competing
with what I'm capable of."[2] Jordan was simply trying to get better
than he was the day before.

Every sport has their arguable GOAT. Tom Brady in football. Tony Hawk in skateboarding. Shaun White in snowboarding. Serena Williams in tennis. Sometimes "Who's the GOAT?" is an internet debate that we love to rehash. Tupac or Biggie? Jordan or LeBron? From Olympic gold medalists to Oprah to Steve Jobs to Walt Disney to John D. Rockefeller to Mark Zuckerberg to Beyoncé to Bono, there are many names who have claimed GOAT status in some arena or another.

Culturally, we are enticed with becoming the best professionally and personally. We want to be the best employee our company has ever had, while simultaneously being the best partner for someone we love, while attempting to be the best parent our kids could ever imagine. Throw in friendships and hobbies, and we've got quite a bit to be the best at.

My son told me the other day that I was the best dad ever and it warmed my heart. Now, he may or may not have said that simply because I gave him candy. And I'm wondering what other father he might have in his life that he's comparing me to. Nevertheless, I'll take it.

When watching the Olympics every four years, people can tell you who won gold. The gold medalists get elusive endorsements and are featured on every morning show and Wheaties box. But no one brags about bronze medals. They don't even really brag about silver. Silver medalists don't get book deals or their images on stamps. You only get to be a hero if you are the best of 7.7 billion.

So what happens when you aren't the GOAT? What happens when you find yourself in the neighborhood of just . . . *great*. "Of all time" is territory very few get to move into. In this chapter, my goal is to help redefine how you think about achieving success, so that success becomes a journey rather than a destination.

Going on a quest to better yourself goes hand in hand with your vision for success. Ideally, you have read chapter 1, done the exercises, and come up with a thoughtful and holistic definition of success for yourself. The problem is that most people often come up with goals that aren't based in reality.

FROM SELF-AWARENESS TO SELF-IMPROVEMENT

I understand the temptation to set the bar for success or failure at "World's Greatest." Beyond sports and entertainment and bestseller lists and being the World's #1 Dad, the GOAT temptation creeps into the corporate world as well. Jim Collins, in his bestselling book *Good to Great*, talks about the importance of BHAGs—Big Hairy Audacious Goals. I like big goals, too, but I often wonder what it's doing to our mental health to constantly fall short of audacious. Sometimes, audacious is exhausting because we never feel like we get a win.

When goals are sky-high, people often fall short. If you never get any wins, you will start to become demoralized. Way too many people are beating themselves up for not being the world's greatest when very few of us are Guinness World Record holders. The standard cannot be "if you're not the best, you're a failure." But what if instead of trying to be the best, you were just better than you were yesterday?

Ryan Holiday, a modern Stoic philosopher and podcaster, says, "Think progress, not perfection."[3] Creating nuance around your goals, shifting the metric from "best" to "better," will do a lot for your mental health and sense of satisfaction.

Asking yourself, "How can I get better?" is a great question for everybody, even people who aren't trying to break sports records or sales records, because it also applies to your relationships. Maybe you need to get better at parenting. Maybe you need to be a better friend. Maybe you need to be more patient with customer service agents. Maybe you just need to be better about calling your mom. Rather than giving yourself a hard time about not being the World's #1 Parent, you can use this question to help you continue to improve as a parent.

The best part about being focused on getting better is that your goals are entirely within your control. If you aren't the best salesperson, you *might* blame it on your performance, but you also might blame it on your customers, the software you are forced to use, bad luck, the economy, and, most of all, your boss. So many of us are sure we would be crushing it if it weren't for the bad leaders standing in our way.

I once consulted with a company that was having trouble with their HR department. From my analysis, it was true that executive leadership was not making HR's job easy. They had put a lot of barriers in place to prevent them from doing their job well. The problem was, when I talked to other leaders at the company, they weren't frustrated with executive leadership, they were frustrated with HR for dropping the ball in areas well within their control.

Employees in the HR department were notorious for not being on time to meetings, for not calling prospective candidates back, and for being sloppy in handling onboarding processes. HR's heart was in the right place—they really did want to create procedures and processes that brought value to all employees—but they were so focused on hurdles with executive leaders that they forgot to be good at the aspects of their job that *were* within their control.

It is always easier to blame someone else for why we are not better, when there are absolutely things we could work on. HR couldn't pursue their strategic plan exactly like they wanted, but they could show up on time to meetings—they didn't need the executive leadership team's permission for that.

Even when there are extenuating circumstances that make your job or life more challenging, you can always ask how *you* can get better. Don't fall for the temptation of fixating on how *they* can get better. This is true in romantic relationships too. *If he were more romantic, I would be. If she were more affectionate, then I would be.* The success of your relationship can't depend on hoping the other person improves. Instead, create a plan for how *you* can improve and make that your metric for success.

People routinely become stuck on all the things they can't control. When we focus our attention on the uncontrollable, we become disgruntled, grumpy, and demoralized. This manifests in many ways. Just like we don't control the future, we also don't control the past. You might have had a bad dad, but that doesn't mean you have to be a bad mom. It also doesn't mean you have to be the best mom to have ever lived. All you need to do is work on being a better parent to your kids than you were yesterday.

We cannot allow someone else's lack of leadership, follow-through, relational IQ, emotional intelligence, passive-aggressive comments, or flat-out aggressive comments to determine the trajectory of where we want to go in our lives.

You may not be able to make your company a better place to work, but you can make yourself a better person to work with. You can't control how your mate improves, but you can improve your part of the relationship. You may not be able to move the dial on diversity and inclusion in the world, but you can become a more diverse and inclusive person.

In circumstances where you control nothing, the only thing you have left to choose is who you want to be and how you can get there one step at a time. This is the magic of self-improvement.

To fully launch your journey to self-improvement, you need to be set up with a few protections from the common pitfalls of people on the path to becoming better.

Wanting to be better is, hopefully, something you undertake

with the best intentions. But growth is uncomfortable, requiring extra vulnerability and introspection. If you read the previous chapter, you have already opened the door to self-analysis and making room for others' perspectives. Now it is time to take it to the next level, moving from self-awareness to self-improvement.

EVERYBODY NEEDS INSURANCE

Becoming a better version of yourself sounds nebulous, but you can be strategic about it, especially if you outfit yourself with the right insurances. I believe there are five "insurances" that asking, "How can I get can better?" offers:

1. Irrelevancy Insurance
2. Ego Insurance
3. Comparison Insurance
4. Offense Insurance
5. Roller-Coaster Insurance

Let's break down how each one can help you level up in your life and career.

Irrelevancy Insurance

What can't you see coming that could derail your professional life?

What's gotten you where you are that may not serve you well with where you're going?

Many of us, in both our personal and professional lives, work hard to get comfortable. But growth requires change, and change is hard. Growing a business requires change. Growing a marriage does too. Most of us avoid change if we can, carving out a niche for ourselves so we can spend the rest of our lives coasting. We'd rather things be consistent. Though that might be nice, one of the cons is that when things never change, we don't either. That can be good in some scenarios but bad for our growth.

When was the last time you learned a new skill? When was the last time you read about a subject that was outside your norm? Most people are naturally intimidated by what they don't understand. Cryptocurrency, NFTs, the metaverse, and TikTok have forced whole generations to think differently. Each of those are worlds with their own unique language that a lot of people won't take the time to understand.

As easy as it is to dismiss any of the above and more, the more dismissive we are of new things, the higher the chances we will find ourselves plateaued, and worse, irrelevant.

Prior to the pandemic, I think we could get away with being on autopilot. Now it's impossible. COVID-19 didn't ask anyone's permission when it upended traditional work-life routines and sent everyone home. Plenty of people get older and wear their inability to use new technology as a badge of honor. But if you didn't figure out Zoom in 2020, you didn't have a job.

In esteemed podcaster, thought leader, and author Carey Nieuwhof's book *Didn't See It Coming*, he outlines the seven major challenges life is guaranteed to throw at us—but somehow, we never expect them. Of the seven, which include personal attributes like cynicism or pride, he also lists irrelevance. Of everything waiting for us, irrelevance is one of the hardest to see in the mirror.

The longer you are in a job, especially if you are good at it, the more likely you are to plateau. You don't think you need to change, innovate, or adjust anymore because you have already had a history of success. Unless your company invests in continuing education or you work in an industry that requires your knowledge base and skill set to grow (e.g., medicine), learning new things won't happen if you don't seek that learning out. Most of us are not good at doing that.

But even at the pinnacle of your career, there is always more to learn and accomplish. You'll know when you have plateaued because, even if you are comfortable and coasting, you might have a slight sense of unease. Maybe you are a little bored. Maybe you are even a little dissatisfied. These are signs you have stopped growing.

This is a question you need to start grappling with inwardly. Even though you have made it, how could you get better? Where are areas for improvement? If your role or your company or the economy shifts majorly again, is your skill set still going to be valued? How do you make sure you are a voice people always want at the table?

In a later chapter we will explore tangible ways to take risks and supercharge growth, but for now sit with the idea that all of us are at risk of becoming dinosaurs if we do not actively seek out growth opportunities. We run this risk in our personal lives as well. Complacency is a killer of marriages and other strong relationships. The best relationships are ones where each party is actively invested in getting better, even when their baseline is pretty great.

You could be a phenomenal husband, mom, boss, teammate, or colleague today, but looking for ways to get better keeps you relevant for tomorrow.

Ego Insurance

How do you make sure your ego isn't preventing you from growing?

There are other reasons why people plateau. One reason I've witnessed, especially at the top, is ego. They have gotten to a place where no one can tell them anything. Ego might try to convince them that they are awesome to be around, always right, and beyond the need to improve.

Fortunately, just by engaging with this chapter, you are opening the door to the possibility that you might still have some growing to do. I will give you even *more* opportunities in chapter 5, which is all about reckoning with what mistakes you want to own. But here is where you start asking yourself whether an inflated sense of self is holding you back.

Oversized egos can be found everywhere, but the more power and success someone has, the more likely they are to be arrogant. People at the top don't get challenged the way others do, and they have a lot of external markers of success to point to and justify why everyone needs to listen to them.

But the more success you have, the more you should be looking for ways to get better. You could be a professional athlete at the top of your game, but being the best in your sport does not make you a good teammate. You could be the smartest doctor in the state and not have compassion for patients. You can create great products but not have quality customer service to deliver them to anyone.

It doesn't matter how good you are at what you do, your success is not a free pass to get out of improving yourself. There's always room for improvement. Looking for ways to get better ensures you don't end up on a pride island where it's your way or the highway.

Some tech visionaries, once-in-a-generation inventors, have bullied their way to the top. They are brilliant but ruthless and willing to bulldoze anyone who gets in the way of their success. Sometimes we can believe the narrative that we need to charge ahead to make things happen at all costs. But what if doing so costs you respect and influence?

Why can't we be really good at our jobs and really good to people at the same time? Outdoor clothing and gear company Patagonia famously takes excellent care of their employees, while also making world-class products year after year. Patagonia calls itself an "uncompany," or a business whose primary concern isn't making money but taking care of its employees, customers, and the environment.[4] Employees get incredible benefits like being able to take two months off (paid) to volunteer with an environmental project, usage of any of the three on-site childcare centers, or a free pass from work when the surf is good. Patagonia will also pay for nursing mothers to bring their baby and a nanny along for business trips. That and they're still the number one performer in the outdoor apparel market.[5] Their values enhance their financial performance instead of detracting from it. But why are they the exception, not the rule?

Let's just say you're a one-in-a-million talent. There's *still* room for you to get insight from outside sources and be amazing. It doesn't make you any less amazing, I've heard.

Ego can be crushing in our personal relationships as well. The number of divorces that have happened because neither side could admit they were wrong has to be hefty. Don't let your ego cost you the relationships that matter the most.

Comparison Insurance

How can you learn from the world around you without losing your way?

Ego can work in the opposite direction though, too, especially when it is partnered with the green-eyed monster: envy.

Envy is always dangerous, but there is a difference between envy and comparison. You can compare yourself to someone else without coveting their lifestyle or achievements. Comparison often gets a bad rap—understandably so in a social media age—but it can be useful. You just have to be very careful how you utilize comparison and keep a constant check if it is causing your focus to slip.

Comparison helps when you are asking the question, "How can I get better?" One form of comparison is noticing things about other people you admire that you can incorporate into your own life. If they are amazing at a specific element of their job or personal development, you can take note of that as something to work on. This is when comparison becomes inspiration.

I spend plenty of time studying other speakers and content creators. My goal is not to *be* the best but to *do my best*. I'm not trying to be the most sought-after speaker in the world. I am just trying to give my best and add value to other people's lives. If I do that well, I'll be a sought-after speaker. But I won't be sought after if I'm not willing to get better at what I do. If someone else is doing something in a creative or efficient way, I want to learn from them or study them. The better I get at my craft, the more people I can help.

But if I find myself looking at their stuff and thinking, *More likes, more books sold, more attention, more events*, then I need to take a break. Knowing all those metrics doesn't make me better at my job. That mindset is a dangerous place to be.

Instead of unproductive comparison, frame the question as, "What they are doing is great, and I'm so glad they're crushing it. Given the excellence on display, how can I get better so that I can progress enough to meet my goals and have the impact I want to have?" By re-grounding yourself in your endgame, you have a recipe to joyfully learn from the world around you rather than constantly being sad about all the success you think you don't have.

Offense Insurance

When you ask for help getting better, how will you receive what people have to say?

Of all the insurances you need to be a better you, this one is key. Getting Offense Insurance allows you to move from working on your growth internally to going externally and incorporating other people in the process. Just like self-awareness, you can only do so much work bettering yourself before you need other people's input and guidance.

Asking other people how you can get better is scary because it puts you in a vulnerable position. Learning how you can get better involves learning where people think you have a weakness or, at best, an area for growth. It is easy to ask for feedback, get it, and then think, *I can't believe they thought that about me!* They're called "blind spots" for a reason.

But other people can hold the secrets to our growth. They can help us see those blind spots and even offer ideas about how to fix them. When you ask someone what it's like to be on the other side of you, it might be difficult for them to give you an honest answer because that's about your personality and how others experience it. However, asking how you can get better helps you evaluate your performance and how you can improve. Sometimes it is not just asking how *you* can get better. Sometimes it is asking how *it* can be better or how *we* can get better.

If you ask the right person, they will not offer a laundry list of your failings. They aren't there to beat you up—they just want to help you figure out how to grow and improve.

Choose wisely when it comes to the family member, friend, or colleague you consult. The best person to ask is the one who is almost reluctant to share their opinion, someone who is both honest and kind. Their ability to be honest will depend on how you handle feedback as well as what is on the line for them should you react poorly.

This is why soliciting feedback in a professional setting has to be approached carefully. If you're the leader, your employees are going to be reluctant to be honest with you because they don't want to lose their job! In order for people with less power than you to be honest with you about what you do or don't do well, they have to have total assurance that they will not have to pay the price for their candor.

It's unfortunate this is true because the best feedback can come from unexpected places. We tend to think we can only get advice from people who are ahead of us in life. When it comes to marriage, we only want advice from people who have been married longer than us. If it's parenting, we only consult people with older kids. If it is our career, we look for mentors and solicit feedback from people several rungs up the ladder with more years of experience under their belts.

If you are only willing to listen to sources you deem credible, you are mathematically reducing your pool of potential people who can help you grow. Never assume people can't offer a valuable perspective just because they don't have twenty years of experience on you or seven more kids.

Sometimes I tell my clients, "The person who has the most to teach you is the one who just got here." A fresh perspective might be just the solution to unwind problems that have been plaguing you. Either they have less invested in keeping the fantasy alive or they have the clarity that comes with no baggage.

Let me put this in perspective: We all have that one relative who hasn't changed their furniture in twenty years, and, as a result, their house smells, and they don't know it. But we smell it when we come by for the holidays. Every organization that's been around for a while has a smelly couch. And a new person who walks in might be the only one willing to be honest about it and the only person who can identify it. You need someone to help you know your couch smells.

I love meeting people who are totally new to me and my content and are willing to offer their fresh perspective. I was listening to a podcast recently that modeled this dynamic well. On organizational psychologist and author Adam Grant's podcast, *WorkLife*, he interviewed Ray Dalio, the incredibly successful CIO of Bridgewater, the world's largest hedge fund. The episode was about how Bridgewater fosters a culture of feedback, and, at the end of the interview, Ray asked Adam how he could get better as an interviewee.

The following conversation took place at the end of the podcast and was fascinating as Adam shared honestly and Ray listened.[6]

RAY: So, now what criticisms do I get?

ADAM: Oh, I have to criticize you?

RAY: Yeah.

ADAM: Ugh. Do we have time for this? [They laugh.]
You stay at the level of abstract concepts and ideas as opposed to moving down into sort of the experiences that you've had, the stories that you can tell, the emotions that are part of that that really bring your ideas to life. If you brought more of the concrete, the emotional, in along with the abstract conceptual, I think your communication would be more effective.

RAY: Well, thank you.

I was impressed with how Ray practiced what he preached in real time with Adam.

One of the pieces of content that has catapulted my career is a documentary called *Chasing Failure* where I tried out for the Phoenix Suns and, indeed, failed. I remember asking my best friend for feedback of the first cut of the documentary. He ripped it apart. He literally suggested I cut it in half. I had an emotional attachment to the project. I was offended by his feedback. We didn't speak for twenty-four hours, but once I got over it, I thanked him. He was right, and his input made the film better.

Now when I ask for feedback in person, I always pull out a notebook or my iPad and write down what the other person is telling me. This signals to them I am taking what they have to say seriously. *I respect you, I value your perspective, and I will take this into consideration.* They could still be wrong, but I'm open to the idea that I'm the one who has it backward. You are literally disarming the bombs of offense when you invite honest feedback this way.

Asking for feedback in order to get better isn't something we do once. It is an ongoing practice with regular check-ins to make sure you are on track for your endgame. This is my primary job as an executive coach: holding people accountable to their goals. I make sure to practice what I preach here, even if it's scary and hard. As I was writing this book, I thought about whose feedback about it would make me nervous. Someone whose feedback I value—but whose feedback I am also kind of scared of. Nevertheless, they'll still get a copy and I'll still get their feedback.

My best friend and I have always had an honest relationship. He cares about helping me be my better self and vice versa. His candor, while challenging (he's a lawyer), has also been fundamental to my growth. I hope he would say the same. When I ask for feedback, he knows the drill. While writing this chapter, I texted him: How can I get better?

Here was his response:

I would love to sit down and talk to Matt Damon because he seems like a good conversationalist, is thoughtful, and doesn't seem to consider himself better than anyone, and is obviously intelligent. But my #1 fear with talking to him is that he would get bored. My life is so boring compared to his. People with more interesting life experiences work as his assistant probably. So if I was sitting across from Matt Damon and he asked me how things were going, I'd be a little oversensitive to any indication he's checking out. I think you can have that effect on people. In general, your life is pretty interesting. You've always met somebody awesome, been somewhere awesome, or done something awesome. So I think people are going to be over-sensitive to whether they are boring you or not. You may not be at all. But they are going to look for it. In general I think you do a great job engaging people, but it's something to be aware of if you weren't.

I sat with his response for a few days, and it was so spot on. In fact, most of the time when I'm done speaking, I'm pretty drained and underwhelming to meet or hang out with. I can easily see someone feeling what he described, and so now I try to go out of my way to make their story more important than mine.

He gave me something to improve in just a text message. It took my friend and me years to build the kind of trust you need to be able to have this exchange, but that doesn't mean you can't start now.

So, here's your homework: Choose three to five people and send them the same text. "How can I get better?" Be strategic about whom you choose: honest, kind, and thoughtful. Not your mom. Not your friend who is just going to respond: "Nothing! You're AMAZING," with seven heart emojis. It's awesome to have fans, but fans don't always help you evolve.

The more you can cultivate an aura that you are willing to receive feedback from the people you trust and invite in, the more it will pay off. There are so many things I have learned about myself that I never would have known if someone hadn't taken the time to tell me. One of my friends told me I walked too fast at events. I thought, "Really, bro? I walk too fast?" Apparently I was unintentionally ignoring people who wanted to talk to me at events, but I never even saw them because I was walking too fast. I would never in a million years have noticed this without my friend telling me.

Now when I walk through lobbies or convention centers, I consciously slow myself down. I hate it. It feels like walking through molasses. It's so much slower, but it's so much better. He was right. People wanted to talk to me, and my speed walking made it seem like I couldn't make time for them. A hard truth had an easy fix, and I am better for it.

Roller-Coaster Insurance

How do I get better without giving in to the highs and lows?

When I was just starting out in my speaking career, I got a lot of feedback, most of it unsolicited. Unsolicited feedback, even when it is well-intentioned and on point, is almost always terrible to receive. No one wants to get critiqued without asking for it. Honesty is always best received by invitation-only. Some pills are hard to swallow, but they go down easier when we're the ones who requested the pills in the first place.

Some of the feedback I got early on was tough (you can read more about it in my book, *Chasing Failure*). It was unsolicited then. But now I look for it. I don't want to miss out on a piece of advice that could help me refine my craft. So now I send an email soliciting feedback from my clients as soon as the event is done.

Preemptively asking for feedback makes it much easier to embrace, especially when I am nervous about what the client is going to say. This is an important element on our collective journeys to betterness: while we need other people to grow, we also have to make sure that harsh feedback—well-intentioned or not—can't torpedo our dreams.

As you try to improve yourself, there will be moments of great triumph balanced out by some real low points. It can be a roller coaster, and you can't get on that ride. It will flip you upside down and in reverse until you have no ability to anchor yourself in the truth of what people are telling you. Half the battle with feedback is knowing what to take and what to leave.

There is temptation in both the highs and lows of the success coaster. The danger of succumbing to the lows is more obvious, but the highs can be just as disruptive. There is a difference between celebrating your wins and getting too into your own hype.

But somewhere between insecurity and arrogance, we're looking for confidence. If we are trying to get better day by day, we are acknowledging we are not perfect and we care about improving. "How can I get better?" keeps you from getting cocky. If it went amazingly and you ask, "How can I get better?" you are keeping yourself focused on improvement. If it went terribly, you are in the same headspace and you can skip the negative self-talk.

If we are honest, none of us like people who are insecure *or* cocky. These attitudes drive us crazy. For every sports legend who couldn't get enough of their own success, there was a team behind the player who hated playing with them, no matter how many rings everyone got. What you're looking for is confidence that can be found in consistent improvement over time. This is not the book where I tell you to become a perfectionist about success. Sometimes better is good enough.

IN CASE YOUR PEOPLE FAIL YOU

I ask myself how I can get better after every book, speech, message, and post. It has become the equilibrium for me. When I think I've killed it, sometimes my clients aren't fans. The social media posts I think could go viral get incredibly low engagement. Other times, I think I bombed, and I get raving reviews. Or the random social post I put up thoughtlessly gets insane amounts of engagement. By viewing everything through the lens of improvement rather than success or failure, the actual successes or failures puff me up or beat me up less.

This question is a powerful one you should be asking yourself when you're stuck. It's even more powerful when you invite some outside sources to help.

Now, let's say you reach out to your three to five people and they don't give you anything you can work on because you are amazing. Here's a short list of things we can all get better at:

- Meetings. (How we plan them. How we engage them. Most people hate them, but it doesn't have to be that way.)
- Listening. (In a society consistently trying to make their voices heard, we can all get better at being quiet. This is particularly useful in marriage and dating too.)
- Empathy. (Putting ourselves in someone else's shoes.)
- Apologizing. (I don't know anyone who's good at this.)

I know we all have a desire to get to the next level quickly. But there are many things you can improve at your current level that will help you prepare for the next level.

So how can you get better? Keep asking yourself that. And then pull some friends into the conversation as well. The next level is that much more within reach if you are receptive to new ways you can improve.

CHAPTER RECAP

- Believing you need to be the GOAT of life is harmful to real self-development.
- Move your metric for success from chasing wins to constant self-improvement.

- To improve, make sure that complacency, ego, comparison, offense, and your highs and lows don't derail you.
- Involve trusted advisors in your journey to get better.

DO THIS NOW

The Feedback Exercise

Ask three to five trusted advisors: How can I get better?

CHAPTER 4

THE TEAM PLAYER QUESTION

What credit can I give away?

*Be generous with your time and your resources and
with giving credit and, especially, with your words. It's
so much easier to be a critic than a celebrator.*
—Maria Popova

The "selfie" industry is booming. Think about it.

Self-care.
Self-help.
Self-worth.
Self-awareness.
Self-talk.
Self-love.
Self-healing.
Self-defense.
Self-employment.
Self-improvement.
Self-leadership.

This book probably falls into half of those categories. I've got entire keynote presentations for six of them. But I think we have to be cautious with how many selfie conversations we have. By constantly being in selfie mode, we run the risk of becoming self-absorbed.

What is even more dangerous than being self-absorbed is actually believing we're *self-made*. This is a selfie that is often coveted and even celebrated.

We love stories about people who started from the bottom and made it to the top. Rags to riches is *the* American dream. Successful people way too often make what they do look easy. To make others feel like the impossible is achievable, some will even share their failures, years where they had to grind, and their upbringing of walking uphill in the snow eight miles to get to work.

When someone has climbed and clawed their way to the top, we hear statements like:

"All I had was me."

"I came from nothing."

"I was broke."

"I was homeless."

"I maxed out four credit cards to get this business off the ground."

"I made all this happen on my own."

And yet I laugh anytime I hear about a self-made billionaire. Why? Because, for starters, whoever that is had a mom. Somebody else biologically made them. As far as their careers go, while they may have had a lot to do with where they've gotten, I guarantee they didn't get there by themselves.

Even the valedictorian from an Ivy League school, who worked hard to be the smartest person in the room, at one point had teachers who helped her get to where she is. Even the successful person who's a high school dropout—at the very least—went to elementary school. I'm sure at some point the person bought a URL for his website. If he used GoDaddy, then GoDaddy helped him.

No matter how self-made someone may think he or she is, I have never met an elementary school drop-out who built web servers from scratch. Every professional athlete had a coach. Somebody in their story gave him or her an introduction. The most self-made person in the world had quite a bit of help becoming who he or she is.

The infamous line from the rapper Drake, "Started from the bottom, now we're here," has often been sung "Started from the bottom and now *I'm* here." But his song says "we're." Which means there's more in his story than just him.

In fact, Drake is a man who did come from humble beginnings relative to the other students at his private school, but those connections afforded him an introduction to the agent who cast him in the Canadian teen drama *Degrassi*, where he got his first big break. He also had a relentlessly supportive mom.[1]

Regardless of the amount of success we accumulate in our lifetime, we must resist the temptation to take all the credit. If you want to grow in your personal and professional life, get in the habit of giving away as much credit as you possibly can. What are we afraid that sharing credit will reveal? Are we worried that admitting we had help will diminish our mystique?

What if you just told the truth: it took a lot of people to get you where you are today—and it will take a lot more to help you achieve the legacy you want for yourself.

GETTING AWAY WITH TAKING CREDIT

Wanting all the credit is not new. Too many times an innovation disrupted the market, a sport, or the way we live, and someone else got all the credit. Then, the rest of us let the thief get away with it. Maybe we never knew the real story, or maybe we did, and we just didn't care enough to fix it.

There are examples of this dynamic across industries and time. Did you know there is a running joke in the scientific community about the discoverers of the DNA helix, James Watson and Francis Crick? It goes something like this: "What did Watson and Crick discover? Rosalind Franklin's notes." Rosalind Franklin's research was given to the two scientists without her permission and proved the key to "their" groundbreaking discovery. They got the Nobel Prize in 1962; she had died of ovarian cancer five years before.[2]

History is full of people stealing ideas and running with them. A great example is Elisha Gray. *Who?* The inventor of the telephone. That's right, *not* Alexander Graham Bell, as we are all taught in elementary school (even if we don't remember that fact in this moment). Not only did Bell not invent the telephone, he actually bribed the patent office to get a peek at Gray's work—and then Gray's patent was conveniently misfiled. And history was made.[3]

Thomas Edison didn't invent the lightbulb either; Heinrich Goebel did and tried to sell it to him. Edison waited until Goebel died, sought out his widow, and bought the patent on the cheap. Then he told everyone the invention was his. He made bank too.[4]

Facebook is an excellent modern-day example. We all think of Mark Zuckerberg as the founder of Facebook. (Unless we saw the movie *The Social Network*—then we know a different story.) The truth is more complicated. Was it just Zuckerberg, or did he really steal the idea from the three founders of ConnectU, the two Winklevoss twins and Divya Narendra? I don't know for certain, but I do know that Facebook Inc. paid $65 million to settle that lawsuit out of court.[5]

Sometimes it isn't just about credit being stolen but the façade of singular success. This is true for musicians, politicians, comedians, and athletes, among many others. Most comedians have an entire team of ten-plus writers behind them. You can bet your favorite singers probably didn't write their biggest hit, and if they did, they probably didn't do it alone. They definitely didn't *record* or market that song alone.

There are too many stories of people who got the credit someone else deserved, or people who took credit alone when they had an army of support, or people who never got any credit at all in both our personal and professional lives. When it comes to real acts of heroism and service, people generally don't need credit—that's how they end up an "unsung hero." But in the rest of our lives, a lack of credit is a real pain point for many of us. We don't feel valued, appreciated, or seen. In fact, this is one of the chief complaints in professional and personal relationships: one party or another feels undervalued. One way you can go to the next level in someone's life is by giving them what most people are not: credit. Because people feel valued when they are given credit.

What accomplishments of yours got appropriated by someone else? How much do you hate being denied credit? What if the person withholding credit is you?

130 PERCENT OF THE PIE

One of the things I see over and over in my executive coaching when I sit with teams is a pain point of people not feeling seen or valued.

How often have we gone to a meeting to share an idea and had it ignored, only to have the same idea brought up by a colleague months later and declared brilliant? How many times have we done the homework only to have it copied? Or made a joke only to hear it repeated later to a rapt audience by the person we told it to? While everyone thinks *they* are hilarious, we know the truth.

I sense that so many people feel undervalued. When we are not given credit over time, we start to become bitter. We can even become grabby about credit. "They're not going to give it, so I'm going to take it." Our impatience with other people's lack of recognition for our contribution becomes very apparent, so much so that others can feel it. Our resentment manifests in our work and in our lives. We see this especially within the realm of marriage.

"I am not a marriage counselor whatsoever," says Gary Chapman. "If you both get in a race for appreciating and apologizing, this relationship will go very far. Most people who are feeling like they're missing something in a relationship, it's that: I wish I had someone who could appreciate the value I bring to it."[6]

When a lack of acknowledgment persists within a marriage—or any relationship, for that matter—it colors every interaction with: "Here's what I'm bringing to the table and you're not." Each spouse will impose their own value system: "I paid for the house" versus "I clean the house." "I watch the kids more than you" versus "I keep the lights on so you can see the kids when you're playing with them." When "my contribution" versus "your contribution" is always being measured, it's hard not to become the resentful party in the marriage.

In our professional lives, when we act this way, we become the odd person out in the meeting. We become the person everyone avoids. Though we might be responding to past circumstances where credit was in short supply, we carry that with us into the future, and we develop a deep-seated bitterness.

On the flip side, we also tend to overestimate the credit we deserve, especially when things are going well. *I'm the reason things are going well*, we often think to ourselves. *It's because of me this is happening.* When I am working with executive teams, I guide everyone through an exercise where they write down the percentage of credit they think they deserve for the company or department's success. The average total number comes back between 130 and 160 percent. There's only 100 percent of a pie to go around, which means people are taking more credit than is even possible to have.

None of us really has an accurate number. We are continually overestimating our contribution and underestimating everyone else's, when really, maybe we are just average. We are better performers than we think we are when we are depressed, and we are not quite as impactful as we think we are when we are crushing it. Most of us lack the ability to assess our actual contribution, so it is best to assume we are somewhere in the middle.

Have you ever heard a leader take credit for what you know to be someone else's work? Whatever you felt in that moment, you want to make sure no one ever feels it about you.

The first step to avoid being a credit hog is to make peace with giving credit away. Leaders especially have trouble with this. They assume that there is a Judas sitting at the table, and if they give that person credit, they will use that humility as leverage. That comes from insecurities. If you are secure in what you do, it is incredible how little you have to worry about the world plotting against you.

I'VE NEVER BEEN ON *OPRAH*

I think we all want other people to believe we are superhuman. Heaven forbid they find out we are actually just human. Or are we afraid that giving credit will take away from our own contribution? This is where confidence once again comes into play. We need to be secure enough to give credit away.

At our most honest, are we afraid people will think less of us if we admit to having help? I run up against this a lot as someone who gets to inspire people around the world through speaking. It is a very rewarding job, especially when it comes to compliments and kind words. But it is always interesting to me to hear people talk about me to their friends and colleagues.

I'll be honest: people exaggerate about me quite a bit. I have heard introductions of me that were so good I thought, *Whoever that mystery person is they're describing, he's about to blow these people's minds, but it's not me.* People have introduced me as a man whose story has been featured on *Oprah* (it was *The Queen Latifah Show*, folks). I've had the wonderful privilege of meeting some incredible individuals; however, Oprah isn't one of them yet—but her name in my intro raises eyebrows. There are moments when I'm tempted to allow an audience to remain impressed with the false intro because what would they think if they knew what I had to say to them that day was sub-Oprah standard?

I also get a lot of good feedback about how my social media content is curated. That's wonderful. I pay people to make those videos and graphics and to curate it. Matt Sandberg along with Zach and Alex Stone are some of the amazing people who create the majority of my video content. I have a team of people who help me think through the content we create for each platform. I wish I could say it was all me, but that's just not true.

When I tell people this, they look a little less impressed—*Oh, he had help?*—but guess what? I did! There were other people involved, and their contributions helped make this YouTube video amazing. I hired a speaker's coach to get better. And guess what? They helped me get to the next level as a speaker. Kelsey Grode helped me with this book. She's an incredible listener, writer, editor, and collaborator. I wish I could tell you I was self-made, but I have had quite a bit of help along my journey. I've actually grown an affinity for people thinking less of me because at least now, if they're thinking of me, they're thinking more accurately of who I actually am.

The funny thing about giving credit away is that, once we get over all our hang-ups, it isn't that hard. What do you lose when you give away credit? It isn't stocks, shares, or money (for most people at least). It is just credit and ego. It is as simple as pointing across the room and saying, "Someone else is responsible for this too."

A few years ago, I was listening to an interview with NBA

legend Allen Iverson. He was talking about his career, including the move that had revolutionized the NBA: the crossover.

As an avid basketball fan, I'm always fascinated with not just players who have Hall of Fame talent but players who *changed the game*. Allen Iverson was one of those players. He is known for pioneering the crossover, a move where a player fakes out the opposing player by switching the ball to the other hand and quickly changing direction.

There is a famous moment in his rookie year where Iverson used the move on Michael Jordan to score. Many sports commentators have called that specific moment iconic. A YouTube video titled "Allen Iverson Crossover" posted by the NBA has millions of views.[7]

Here's the thing: Allen Iverson didn't come up with the crossover move himself. Dean Berry, his college teammate at Georgetown, taught it to him. That's right—who? Allen Iverson went on to change the game of basketball after college. Dean Berry became an executive at a medical supplies company.

Larry Platt, in his 2002 book, *Only the Strong Survive*, wrote about how Berry changed the game. He was a "cerebral" player and had analyzed hours of tapes, putting together the steps that different players did best to ultimately come up with . . . the crossover.[8]

"He was killing me every day in practice, so I finally asked him to show me how to do the move," said Iverson.[9] Just like that, Iverson pulled back the curtains on the move that had become his legacy—and gave the credit away.

When I heard those words come out of his mouth, I was shocked. The crossover was Iverson's *thing*. The term "breaking ankles" literally comes from him! Yet twenty years later, he went and gave the credit to someone else. And it doesn't make him any less of a hall of famer because of it.

What you lose when you give away credit is . . . nothing. What you gain when you give it away is respect. How good does it feel when you are seen and valued? When your contribution is brought to the table? How awesome does it feel to work for, work with, or be married to the person who gives credit away? We all love being around those people, and, at some point, we have to decide to be that person.

FOLLOW THE BREAD CRUMBS

The most underrated component of my life and career is my wife. She is introverted, neither loud nor boisterous. She is not out there or in your face. We are not the selfie couple. We go on dates a lot, but we rarely, if ever, post photos. We go on nice vacations. If we take photos on those vacations, they stay on our phones.

Most people have no idea how much of my success can be credited to my wife and how well she holds down the fort at home when I travel. They would be shocked by how much of my content derives from conversations we've had, especially the digital content that gets the most engagement.

In 2020, I began doing more virtual keynotes like everyone else. I needed a background that was going to look amazing. My wife is an interior designer and so she created a virtual studio space in our home office that looks incredible. After I would finish a virtual presentation, clients would often request a follow-up meeting just to learn about how everything was set up.

Whenever I receive compliments about our virtual setup, it would be easy for me to say, "Thanks!" Instead, I tell them, "Actually, my wife designed the whole thing. She's brilliant and creative. Y'all should schedule a Zoom with her, not me." And do you know what that costs me? Nothing.

At some point, you have to get to a place where you can think, *I don't need to be that impressive. I don't need to be hailed, esteemed, or adored. It is better to share that spotlight with the team or the people in my life who deserve it. Everything I have has an army of support and love behind it.*

One of the tools I often use in my corporate keynotes is what I call the "bread crumb slide." It is a slide with all the names of people who helped me get to the point of receiving that exact opportunity. I follow the bread crumbs all the way back to a ninth-grade English teacher who paid for me and my brother to stay in a private school. That allowed me to meet a coach who allowed me to go to college that allowed me to meet my first employer who allowed me to start my career speaking to a group of ten who allowed me to speak to a group of ten thousand who allowed me to meet an agent who now allows me to speak all around the world.

My audience ends up looking at a slide of names that appear one by one that have no meaning to them until they see the last name that pops up—their CEO or meeting planner. I tell the story of who introduced us and how we met. Then everyone realizes that I'm only in the room because of a long line of people who gave me a chance to succeed.

From there I give the company a five-to-ten-minute opportunity to start giving away credit. Each person has to shout out one person in the company. It turns into a credit party. Here's what happens every single time: someone gets seen who had no idea anyone was thinking so highly of them.

At the end of movies, there are always credits. At the end of this book, there will be acknowledgments. Life would be better if we lived that way too. Who belongs in your credits? Take five minutes and write down the names of the people who were most influential in getting you where you are. This is your own bread crumb slide. Then, text them and tell them thank you.

This might be your husband. This might be your wife. It could be your boss or an intern. It could be a parent. It could be a friend. It could be a roommate. Your bread crumb slide is yours.

Once you have it, think about the people in your daily life. I am sure there are many people who deserve to hear from you about how their contributions, big and small, are responsible for your success. Who are the unsung heroes of your life? How are you going to make sure they feel that appreciation from you?

All of us need to genuinely analyze our bread crumb slide. Beyond a thank-you text, what kind of credit do these people deserve? Does it need to be public? Private? A card? Money? How do you make sure that the people who matter most in your life feel your gratitude?

CHAPTER RECAP

- Being "self-made" is a myth; everyone had help getting where they are today, no matter what we want to believe about ourselves.
- People have a hard time giving credit away and tend to take more credit than they deserve. Err on the side of generosity when it comes to giving away credit.
- The biggest cost of giving away credit is pride.
- Make a practice of giving credit, praise, and gratitude.

DO THIS NOW

The Bread Crumb Exercise

Create your own bread crumb slide. Working backward, trace how you ended up with the current opportunities you have. Who is responsible for getting you in the room? Bonus points if you reach out and thank them.

CHAPTER 5

THE HUMILITY QUESTION

What mistakes can I own?

Is it too late now to say sorry?

—Justin Bieber

On a cold Wednesday in December, my son Jaxson and I were driving home trying to figure out what we were going to eat for dinner.

> **ME:** Jaxson, what would you like for dinner?
>
> **JAXSON:** A cheeseburger with meat and cheese only from Whataburger.
>
> **ME:** Okay, sure.
>
> **JAXSON:** Actually, I want a cheeseburger *with gummies.*

At this point in our conversation, I felt insulted. What respectable establishment, in their right mind, would put gummies on a cheeseburger?

> **ME:** Jaxson, there is no such thing.
>
> **JAXSON:** Yes, there is. I want a cheeseburger with gummies.
>
> **ME:** Jaxson, they do not have a cheeseburger with gummies, nor should they!
>
> **JAXSON:** Can you please just ask?

Now we had to settle the score. Who was right? Who was wrong? Only the cashier at Whataburger could settle this debate.

However, the mere fact that I'd have to ask another contributing member of the American economy if they had a cheeseburger with gummies felt beneath me. At the same time, I was sure they'd had crazier requests. Despite my better judgment, I rolled up to the drive-through and went for it.

> **ME:** Hi, um, hey, do you guys happen to have . . . a
> cheeseburger . . . with gummies? You know, like
> gummy worms or gummy bears?
> **WHATABURGER EMPLOYEE** (laughing): No, sir, we do not.

My son sat in the back seat disappointed with life, and I was, indeed, correct: Whataburger does not serve a cheeseburger with gummy bears, gummy rings, or any other kind of gummies on it. But I didn't gloat over my victory. Instead, I simply continued on with a very normal food order.

> **ME:** No problem, man. Can I get a kid's cheeseburger,
> meat and cheese only, with a lemonade to drink?
> **WHATABURGER EMPLOYEE:** Alright, and for the kid's
> snack, would you like a cookie or fruit chews?

Fruit chews? Also known as *gummies* to an eight-year-old?

What a comeback win by Jaxson, and he didn't even realize it until we got home. I wish I could say he was as gracious about proving me wrong. Whataburger does in fact sell gummies, which they call "fruit chews"; they're just not actually *on* their cheeseburgers.

Now let me ask you: Who was right in that situation? Me, Jaxson, or the Whataburger employee? I could make the argument for either, but for the sake of this chapter, let's put this one on me.

Isn't it interesting how many miscommunications we experience at work and at home? These could be caused by an email, text, or phone conversation where there is a rather large chasm between what you said and what the person on the receiving end heard, or vice versa. In those moments our inclination is to blame the other parties involved. But the real growth for us lies with owning our part.

Singer-songwriter Billy Joel says it like this: "You're not the only one who's made mistakes, but they're the only things that you can truly call your own."[1]

When things are going well, people can't wait to take credit. But as soon as things start going badly, everyone can't wait to point fingers and place blame.

This is the *ownership* chapter. Just like you learned how to give credit in the last chapter, this chapter will help you take responsibility for the mistakes you need to own. Next-level people have no problem giving away credit or taking the blame.

As I have gotten older, I've realized that in every situation where I have had a personal or professional rift, gotten into a conflict, or had bitterness toward someone, there has been only one common denominator: me.

It would be easy to sit back and think, *Those people are idiots. I am awesome, and they are the problem.* Remember, we tend to overestimate our contributions and underestimate the harm we do. But the reality of our always being right and/or wronged is highly unlikely. So why do we want to think we are the victims of everyone else's bad behavior? Probably because, if giving credit away is difficult, taking ownership is even harder.

When you give credit, it involves words like "Thank you." But taking ownership involves words like "I'm sorry," the two most difficult words in the English language. Maybe yours are: "My bad," "This one's on me," "That's my fault," or "That's my oversight." Apologizing can feel like waving the white flag. It equates to: "You're right, and I'm wrong." No one wants to surrender that. We would much rather project blame or make excuses.

I have made so many mistakes over the course of my career. One month I accidentally double-booked keynotes to speak for two large companies on the same day and didn't realize it. I was completely embarrassed. My friend was like, "Blame it on COVID-19" (which I had contracted at the time). I couldn't. As much as I wanted to say I'd gotten sick and my schedule and mind got twisted, that wasn't the truth. I messed up, and it was on me. Which is what I said when I called and apologized profusely to my literal biggest client.

So, what if we just owned up? How many times have you been late and blamed it on traffic? Was it really traffic? Can you imagine if someone was brutally honest about their tardiness?

"I'm sorry I'm late. I didn't like what I was wearing. There are eight outfits on the floor."

"I'm sorry I'm late. I just wanted to see the end of a YouTube video."

"I'm sorry I'm late—the line was really long at Starbucks."

When companies started giving their employees the option to work remotely, making excuses for being late got harder. Being on time to a meeting was just a matter of pressing a button. Traffic and wrong turns don't work as excuses for Zoom, but we still try. I used to blame my children a lot. Today I was one minute late for a meeting. I would have loved to say that my internet was slow, or my computer was finishing an update, but the reality was that my kid walked in, grabbed my hand, and pulled me down to talk to him. *I can't rush this child,* I thought.

And so, I was late. Just by one minute, but still late. Instead of lying or making excuses or even blaming my kid, I told the executive I was coaching that my son needed me for a second. I owned it, and he totally understood.

I think we are afraid that if we own our mistakes and short-comings, people will think less of us. This is especially true with leaders. If they admit that they're wrong, then their teams may think their leader is not worth following. I love what author and speaker David Horsager says in his book *Trusted Leader: 8 Pillars That Drive Results*: the number one question everyone is asking about you is, "Can I trust you?"

Isn't that true of most of us? Whenever we're working with or living with someone, we're wondering how much we can or cannot trust them. What happens when we own up to our mistakes is actually the opposite of what we think will happen: people gain respect for us because they'd rather work with and be with someone who can be honest about their flaws than someone who's pretending they don't have any.

FOUR LITTLE WORDS THAT COULD CHANGE YOUR LIFE

If there is one superpower we all have, it is the ability to see other people's flaws while at the same time lacking total awareness of our own. That mistake you think you are hiding? People know. They might not be totally accurate in their diagnosis, but they are close.

Because people are aware of our mistakes, the more we refuse ownership, the more personal and professional rifts we will have. The people around us chalk up our unwillingness to be wrong to manipulation, cowardice, or, largely, ego. An environment becomes extremely toxic when mistakes and hurts go unaddressed.

Coaching people toward taking ownership begins not by pushing them to apologize but by opening a door in their minds just a crack to the idea that *they might be wrong*. This is the core concept behind *intellectual humility*. It's the importance of knowing that there's a chance, big or small, that you could have made an error. Instead of moving through the world assuming we all have it figured out, what if we navigated the world and conversations with four little words: *I could be wrong.*

Intellectual humility is not a culturally popular value. We are trained to be right. In school, we are penalized for being wrong. We are taught not to make mistakes. One hundred is the goal. As we get older, the more credentials we garner and the grander the titles we are given, the more certainty we think we must cultivate. And the less willing we become to admit we are wrong.

In science, a field where people have alphabets of letters behind their names, there is a problem called "replication crisis."[2] Incredible discoveries are made, researchers publish their results and receive all kinds of coverage and awards . . . and then nobody can follow their process and get the same results. Actually, according to one study, most published scientific results are only replicable 40 percent of the time.[3] Sounds like there might be more room for error than everyone might want to believe, but scientists have a hard time admitting that they could be wrong.

One psychologist, Julia Rohrer, even created a forum called the "Loss of Confidence" project where fellow researchers could share instances of when they had made mistakes.[4] Another researcher, Julia Strand, was inspired by her own experience of trusting the results of a simulation only to discover later she had messed up one line of code. Despite wide coverage and an anonymous survey wherein half the respondents reported knowing they had made scientific mistakes, only thirteen people publicly shared their responses.[5] We really, really don't like to admit when we're wrong.

Carol Tavris is a social psychologist who, with co-author Elliot Aronson, wrote an entire book on being wrong—*Mistakes Were Made (but not by me)*—which explains that there are several reasons we have trouble embracing intellectual humility. Most of us believe we are discerning, thoughtful people. When we are challenged, we look for information that supports our views rather than rethinking our position.[6]

This behavior is called "confirmation bias." We dig in our heels because we are totally invested in our self-image of being "smart, moral, and right." Ironically, the way we approach being those things makes us none of them. In our increasingly digital world, my observation is that people have doubled down on their beliefs because the internet provides so many opportunities to gather evidence and confirm what we already think.

In my work, I travel all around the country and consult with all kinds of people. I see rifts evolving between leaders and their employees, parents and their children, husbands and wives, Californians and Texans—all you have to do is find people on opposite sides of the aisle and you'll see how deep the division has become. Everyone has evidence for why the other person is wrong. Even if we are not saying we are right, we are talking like we are.

When did we all become experts in everything? Especially in the last few years, I have so many friends who have suddenly become medical and epidemiological savants. They have no degrees in science, but they are certified blog readers and believe that hobby gives them scientific credibility. (We all have a friend in the medical field, right?)

Every four years, people become political pundits and electoral statisticians. Election season rolls around, and half the country is shocked when things don't go their way and is frustrated with the other half. I'm astounded by the number of people I know who aren't on speaking terms with their parents or colleagues over heated conversations around politics. I have to wonder if there would still be a relationship there if their conversations made space for the other person's perspective.

Can you imagine what the world would look like if we all had a little more intellectual humility? What if, instead of entering a conversation charged with a viewpoint shaped by our identity and googling, we started by saying, "I could be wrong, but this is my perspective"?

Our conversations would be so much more palatable. The aura in schools, hospitals, offices, and homes would improve. Did you know there is a version of every relationship you have where you can disagree and love each other at the same time? Did you know you don't have to lose friends every election season? What if you went into those conversations saying, "I could be wrong, and I know we don't see things the same way, but I still value you as a person and want to hear what you have to say."

"I could be wrong," means, "I'm making a little room for humility and someone else's perspective." How much would you appreciate being on the receiving end of that qualification? Remember, I'm not asking you to apologize to anyone (we'll get there). But it's going to be very difficult to ever own any mistakes if you don't believe you're even capable of making them. If you can't say, "I *could be* wrong," how could you ever own up to something enough to say, "I *am* wrong"?

THE COST OF ALWAYS BEING RIGHT

What's so bad about being wrong? Why do we have an obsession with being right? Why do we feel like we win a gold medal if we're able to tell someone else, "I told you so"? How many times in your life have you met someone looking for a mate who said, "The kind of person I want to be with is someone who's always right"? You haven't. For the sake of the relationships we have in our homes and in our careers, I believe we have to pause and wonder what it is we win for being right.

I know what we could lose for having to be right all the time: those same relationships. Sometimes you win the argument and lose the relationship in the process. No one wants to work with you. No one wants to raise kids with you. No one wants to be on your team. Was it worth it?

Too many conversations end with our feeling like we have to choose between waving the white flag or dying on a hill. Neither of those extremes feel like options that improve the quality of our relationships. But intellectual humility does.

We can all be smart, but we often become a little too smart for our relationships. Most of us think making room for our own fallacy is the same as surrendering. But admitting you could be wrong doesn't mean you are. There should always be space for more than just your own perspective.

It is possible for me to be wrong and you to be wrong too.

It is possible for me to be right and you to be right too.

One executive might say that the company needs to focus more on recruiting talent, while another believes the organization should double down on retaining talent. They both might be right.

This dynamic shows up in personal relationships too. One parent says, "We need to go on more dates," and the other one says, "We need to spend more time with the kids." They both might be right.

"You *always* say . . ." is usually met by, "Well, *you* always . . ." At some point we have to wonder why we are fighting so hard to win arguments when winning isn't key to any thriving relationship. The key to peace in all of our most important relationships is give and take.

We could all use a little more *relational humility*. What if, instead of saying, "You always . . ." we said, "I'm trying to balance everything—kids, work, our marriage. I could be wrong, but what if our next step is therapy?" What if, instead of saying, "My candidate is the only choice," we said, "I could be wrong, but I think what our country needs is . . ."?

When the people in our lives and at our work know we are willing to be wrong, it is a game changer. The phrase, "I could be wrong," has the power to change the world.

Relational humility at work can sometimes get a little more complicated. Maybe there are stakes to being wrong, especially if you are in charge. Leaders often have something to lose when they make the wrong call. The president can't just go to the podium and apologize without causing international incidents. But we are not the president. We are colleagues, parents, friends, and neighbors.

What I have seen in any organization I have worked with is that all presidents think they are *the* president. The more successful a person is, the less likely they are to admit mistakes. The higher they climb, the harder they fall. They act like they have no margin for error. However, though the stakes may be high, they're still human.

If no one in an organization is willing to be wrong or own their mistakes, people will always be looking for a fall guy. Someone has to take the blame, and we don't want to be that person. Even if it's technology's fault or just bad luck, someone has to take the blame.

Perhaps you've been thrown under the bus at work. Many people know how that feels. It can happen so fast. Before you realize what's happening, you wonder, *How did I get here?*

I believe it's up to the rest of us to stop the bus. Having relational humility at work means that no one needs to be the fall guy, because rather than running someone over, we are willing to get on the bus and chat. We decide how we are going to move the bus forward together.

Unfortunately, when we're afraid, we disallow room for error, refuse ownership, and project blame. Most likely, we are afraid someone is going to blame us. Those behaviors stem from insecurity. Rather than look for villains, we can allow others to see us as we really are: human.

If we are refusing to own mistakes because we fear others will think less of us, maybe others thinking less of us is a good thing. Perhaps we need to model the willingness to be wrong, imperfect, and flawed.

What mistakes do you need to own? Is there anything you could apologize for?

If you're able to tell me that nothing is on you, then I will sell my business right now and come work for you. I would like to work for a perfect person.

In the event you are not a perfect person (I've never met one), then you can bet people will want to work with you, live with you, and be in your life more when you are someone who is willing to own their mistakes.

HOW TO OWN IT

The value of hindsight is that it teaches you how to look backward and analyze your behavior. It is much easier to answer, "Have you ever made a mistake?" versus "What mistakes are you making now?" Saying, "I *was* wrong," is always simpler than admitting, "I *am* wrong." Or "Ten years ago I really messed up," rather than "I was wrong earlier today." We don't feel the consequences of ten years ago—or we think we don't.

The problem is that the moment passes. We hurt someone's feelings. They form an opinion of us or our character. A rift occurs. If we wait too long, even the most genuine apology cannot fix it. How many people would still be married today if they had just said, "I was wrong, and I am wrong. Most of all, I am sorry." Those words look simple on paper, but they can be very difficult out loud.

I think we should be quick to give credit and quick to own our behavior. I also believe we should be slow to take credit and slow to place blame.

Do not wait to apologize when you have done harm. Remember: we are all very aware of others' mistakes. Someone will know if you wait one year, two years, three years to apologize. And during that time, they won't respect you. You will lose out on your relationship with them.

When things are going badly, you should be the first person to say, "Let me take some ownership of where this fell apart and come up with some solutions to fix it." "I could have done this better." "I could have provided clarity in what I was expecting." This isn't about beating yourself up; it's about owning where you fell short. You are taking responsibility.

If you can move swiftly on owning your mistakes and showing your flaws, you help eliminate the chance for resentment. You do not give it time to fester and poison the relationships, both personal and professional, that matter most to you.

Timeliness is just one component of owning mistakes. We also all need some level of awareness of what it is we are owning. You can't take responsibility if you don't know what you're apologizing for. An apology doesn't matter if it isn't genuine.

Remember that we all overestimate how much credit we deserve, but we also probably underestimate how much ownership we need to take. It is better to err on the side of ownership. Are you 90 percent responsible? More like 70 or 30 percent? Whatever number you think you deserve, pretend it's a lot more.

Unlike giving credit, you should not make an inventory of your mistakes. Do not bread crumb your mistakes. Do not make a list of people to text. Instead, think of one person to whom you may owe an apology. Just one.

If you don't think there is anyone to apologize to, my question is, Are you that amazing? It is impressive that there is not one person you need to apologize to. Do you work with people? Have a family? Have friends? And still there's nothing you need to own? You don't have one "my bad"?

I can't guarantee that owning your mistakes or apologizing will always go well. Some people are harsh about receiving apologies, especially some bosses. But the more you own your mistakes, the easier it gets. Acknowledging what you need to own brings humility into the room.

The other day I was presenting. Before my keynote, I had given the media team my notes to put on the confidence monitor. I was doing multiple messages for them, so they had been sent a batch of my notes all at once. I got onstage, started speaking, and you can guess what happened next: the wrong notes had been loaded on the monitor. I then proceeded to give an entire speech from memory as best as I could.

Around the twenty-five-minute mark, twenty minutes before I was supposed to be done, I had said all I could, and I wrapped it up.

"That was good!" people said afterward. "Short, but good."

The media team was mortified. "We are so sorry," they said.

"No, that's on me," I told them. "I should have done a more thorough rehearsal."

We started fighting in the back. I was making the argument that it was on me and they were making the argument that it was on them. It was one of the best fights I've ever had. That's how it should work when everyone takes ownership. Mistakes happen, but nobody is mad at anybody because everyone is committed to playing their part better and are humble enough to admit when they have fallen short. That's the culture you create when everybody owns their part, whether it is praise or blame.

Still, there will be times when you feel like you are the only one owning your mistakes and no one else is. Sometimes you apologize, anticipating the other person to own their part, but instead, they either accept your apology and move on, or worse, they give you a few other things you should be apologizing for. This makes taking ownership incredibly challenging.

However, owning your mistakes isn't about their development, it's about *yours*. You are the one who's trying to take your life and career to the next level. If others around you don't want to do the same, don't let that stunt your growth.

"Admitting mistakes, taking ownership, and developing a plan to overcome challenges are integral to any successful team," writes Jocko Willink in his book *Extreme Ownership*. When things go awry and you say, "This is on me," your healthy team members, family members, or friends are able to say, "Nope, it's on us too."

At the end of the day, in the owning-your-mistakes kind of culture, I should give you grace when you've missed the mark and you should do the same for me. None of us wants to be friends with, work with, work for, or be married to someone who can always see what's wrong with everyone else but cannot acknowledge his or her own shortcomings. We don't want to be around that person, and we should make it our aim not to be that person. This is how we create workplaces, schools, communities, and homes that are both tolerable and nurturing for all our growth.

CHAPTER RECAP

- In every conflict or altercation we have been involved in, we are the common thread.
- The four words that could change the world are "I could be wrong."
- Be slow to take credit and quick to apologize.

DO THIS NOW

Think through your personal and professional relationships and consider owning any mistakes you may have made in the last month.

CHAPTER 6

THE POTENTIAL QUESTION

What risk do I need to take?

Success is stumbling from failure to failure
with no loss of enthusiasm.
—Winston Churchill

Have you ever played The Game of Life? This board game is the one where you are given a little car and then proceed along the track through exciting life events like getting married (add another peg to your car), having a kid (add a smaller blue or pink peg depending on if it's a boy or girl), and buying home or auto insurance (thrilling).

I was reading an article recently by a woman in her late twenties who had played the game and was shocked by how little The Game of Life reflected her own life. Single, twenty-nine, no kids, and no home. No knock on her—she loved her life—but she was surprised by how much she had taken the American dream for granted as her destiny. Her actual life barely resembled what she had been taught to expect.

When The Game of Life was created in 1960,[1] a nice house in the suburbs, two kids, and a linear career path at the same company for thirty years before you retired at fifty-five were pretty much guaranteed.[2] Back then, the median price of a home was $11,900,[3] college (tuition, room and board, and fees) cost about $2,015 a year,[4] and most people had their first kid at twenty-three.[5]

Nowadays, will anyone ever get to retire before Social Security runs out? Most millennials believe they will work part-time into retirement.[6] The current median price of a home is $374,900,[7] college costs $35,331 a year,[8] and millennials are pushing parenthood further and further down the road, to age twenty-six for women and thirty-one for men.[9] For previous generations, people could show up to work, whether at an office or on a farm, put in an honest day, and go home assured that their jobs and careers were set. Loyalty equated to safety. No need to risk anything. Just follow all the steps and you'd likely end up with what most people considered success, including a long and easy retirement full of cruises and grandkids.

Who believes that now?

The world has changed and continues to change. The last hundred years have seen an acceleration of technological progress unlike any time before, especially with a little thing called the internet. Disruption, innovation, and globalization are the name of the game. Even if you had somehow managed to bury your head in the sand for all the years leading up to now, the COVID-19 pandemic changed things for everyone, and it didn't ask anybody's permission.

It would have been great in December 2019 if somebody had called us and said, "Get ready to stay home a lot. Brush up on your math and history because you're about to become your kids' teacher, PE coach, and principal. All this will test your sanity; however, your online meetings using a medium called Zoom will allow you to wear sweatpants to work every day. But you will need to look somewhat presentable from the waist up."

And yet it didn't matter how much you liked change or how loyal you were. In July 2020, 16.9 million were unemployed,

57 percent of whom were unable to work because their businesses closed permanently or had to dramatically scale back.[10] No amount of loyalty or excellent performance was going to fix that. Work-life balance changed dramatically overnight. If you couldn't figure out Zoom, you were out of a job (if you were lucky enough to have one). If you couldn't figure out algebra, your kids weren't going to learn it.

Even knowing which behaviors were risky and which weren't was a total toss-up. Researchers, doctors, politicians, and leaders of all stripes couldn't agree. How did we decide which risks we needed to take in order to keep life functioning at some minimum level? Which risks were the ones that could end it all? Our calculus around how to integrate risk into our everyday lives became a daily practice.

In the middle of the pandemic, I released my book *Chasing Failure*. I was nervous as I started promoting it. Was now really the time to be telling people to open themselves up to new experiences and go after big dreams? Your dreams don't matter if you don't survive long enough to chase them.

What I learned, as the months unfolded, was that doing nothing could be just as risky as trying anything. The people (and organizations) who thrived during the pandemic—or just made it work—were the ones who acclimated themselves to change, rolled with the punches, took calculated risks, and tried again in the face of failure.

There are no more conventional ladders or paths or steps that guarantee success and safety. We must learn to ignore our instinct to hunker down and wait until the storm passes. The storm is not passing. This just might be your life as we know it. Some people are still mourning the life they had BC (Before COVID). But it's going to be hard to level up in your life or career if you don't embrace the here and now.

We have no way of predicting how events will continue to unfold on a world stage and how that will affect our work, our lives, our communities, and our homes. It's wise for us to reframe our thinking to expect change and also prepare for it. When change comes—and it will—how are you going to respond? Where will you find your bravery and willingness to try something new and persist, even when faced with failure?

What I've found is that most people who are stuck at their current level haven't taken a risk in a long time.

CHANGE FATIGUE

Burnout. Exhaustion. Fatigue. Those are the words that fall under the umbrella of the overwhelming tiredness sweeping across the world. What are we tired of, though? What's this fatigue we keep having conversations about?

For some, it is indeed physical. Your body is actually exhausted. For others, it's emotional or mental. Your brain needs a break (more on this in chapter 10: The Rest Question). But what the past couple of years have forced us to do more than ever is *change*. And now we've got *change fatigue*.

Maybe we never liked change to begin with. Maybe we love it, but life has a tendency to allow an overwhelming chaos to creep in, and it can put us in a place where we crave reprieve and could really use a break. Maybe all you want to do is lie low for a while, turn off the news, and never have to update your iOS again.

If you are feeling this way, you are not alone. Organizations from Johns Hopkins to McKinsey have published heavily researched articles about how to overcome burnout and pandemic fatigue.[11] The message is clear: collectively, we have a very hard time consistently adjusting to the new circumstances of our lives, personally and professionally. At home and at the office, consistent restructuring can knock on our doors and upend our routines.

When I work with organizations, one of the top complaints I hear over and over from leaders is that their teams are having a hard time adjusting to change. This is ironic, considering that research shows most leaders *overestimate* how much their employees can handle change. A 2016 survey of over two thousand professionals showed that top-level executives believed just 37 percent of people generally like to remain in the status quo, with a stalwart 63 percent generally wanting to reach for something "bigger and better."[12] Yet only 45 percent of their employees agreed with that assessment. Change is unpopular, especially when it is being pushed on us.

Change fatigue is a different kind of exhaustion. It is an exhaustion of the soul. The world keeps changing, and eventually, even good change feels hard. Our jobs keep changing. Schools keep changing. Technology keeps changing. Plans keeps changing.

But what all this change has forced us to do is try new things and step out of boxes we normally never would.

I actively work to bring change into my life, and even I get tired of it. I get tired of always being the guy at the table asking people to try new things or think differently. I call it "challenger fatigue." You can be the person pushing change and still get really sick of it. You get tired of being uncomfortable, even when that discomfort is good for you.

"Change is the only constant in life," said Heraclitus, a Greek philosopher.[13] A lot has changed since he was kicking it around Ephesus in the 400s BCE, and more change will come.

Change is unavoidable, even if we don't like it and even if we resist it. Change becomes easier when we accept it is coming and meet it head on. If you want to move from where you are to where you want to be, there's going to be a risk you need to take that requires change.

"WE DON'T DO THAT HERE"

Have you ever pitched a new idea that was met with, "We don't do that here," or "That's not how it works," or "It's not how things are done." The personal version of that is, "That's just not me," or "You do you, and I'll do me."

How many times, whether it was your manager, your mom, or your fifth-grade teacher, have you been told "it" isn't possible just because "it" doesn't follow the current program? How did that feel? Frustrating, I am guessing.

"We don't do that here" is a classic. I hear it all the time in the organizations I speak to and consult with. If I'm invited in, I'm not paid to be there to help an organization stay the same. I'm invited there to foster growth and innovation. So, I'm given permission to ask questions out loud that someone else might get fired for.

When I hear "That's just not us" or "We don't do that here," I respond kindly with, "You don't do that here? Is it . . . illegal?"

More often than not, the question I am asking is, "Why?"

The answer is usually blank stares.

I think we grow so accustomed to our way of doing things that we don't know why we're doing them anymore. Sometimes we don't know why we're *not* doing new things. If you have any variation of "We don't do that here" in your office or life, is it possible that you are doing everything in your power to keep everyone inside a box?

I believe out-of-the-box problems require out-of-the-box solutions. For example, supply chain was an issue for almost every business I worked with during this time. Some executives were more creative than others in figuring out solutions. They didn't do anything illegal, but they brought their best minds together to create unconventional solutions that worked.

3M, the multinational conglomerate that makes everything from ScotchTape to sophisticated electronics, produced the N95 mask. As demand surged and the supply chain went off the rails, 3M began taking immediate and drastic steps to ensure production could continue and demand was met. They worked with governments to lower trade barriers, published prices on masks to limit price gouging, fired distributors that raised those prices, set up a hotline for consumers to call to verify their 3M products were legit and not knockoffs, secured their supply chain to stop any leakage to the black market, and had over seven thousand fake websites selling their masks shut down.

They made over two billion N95 masks in 2020, 300 percent of their 2019 production, partially because they had learned from the SARS outbreak in 2002–2004 and built what they called "surge capacity" into every one of their global manufacturing facilities, building assembly lines that are inactivated until demand surges—at no additional impact to their bottom line.[14] They had seen the risk in not being able to handle change—and had learned from their experience.

As a public speaker, I had to go virtual in the pandemic. You can imagine what happened to the speaking and events industry in March 2020. I went from traveling every week to sitting in my chair behind my desk with no timeline on when work would return to normal, if ever.

I have a background in filmography, so I was fortunate enough to have a nice setup at home with the help of my wife. A camera, a microphone, good lighting. Clients would tell me we had to cancel the scheduled event, and I would always offer a virtual alternative. I also made sure clients booking me for a future live event knew that a virtual option was on the table too.

A surprising number of clients had a hard time wrapping their heads around digital events. It's normal now, but when it was new, it didn't fit their idea of what it meant to bring in a speaker. But they wanted to keep everyone safe, and having a space for people to reflect and get some inspiration was critical in surviving a messy year. If I hadn't quickly pivoted to a virtual setup, my speaking business would have remained closed for a very long time. Some people didn't make the shift, preferring to wait it out until live events returned. But no one knew when that would be. How many variants can one virus have?

To open ourselves up to good risk, we first must learn what limiting beliefs are holding us back. Where in our lives have we turned on autopilot? What do we like to tell people we're not good at? Is it true, or are we just afraid to try something, fail, and try again? Where are we stopping ourselves from growing, personally and professionally, because we have accepted the status quo? In turbulent times, it can feel like we need to hunker down. But refusing to change with the times is far riskier than rising to meet the occasion and trying new things.

THE COST OF DOING NOTHING

What 2020 taught us is that some businesses embraced change. Others didn't. Some businesses thrived. Others closed. The ones that thrived were the ones that tried something new. Others stayed in their lane, and sometimes their lane disappeared.

You may not have many choices, but one you do have is whether you will level up or stay put. When faced with tough situations, we often are tempted to hide, avoid, or do nothing. Sometimes doing nothing is the best option, at least in our change-averse minds. But doing nothing is never free.

I saw a tweet that hit this idea home: "somethin kinda neat i found out . . . if you ignore a problem for long enough, it either goes away or ruins your life. so 50/50. pretty good odds," wrote @bobby (Twitter bio: "the goat of all time"—good for you, Bobby).[15]

I don't know about the forty-eight thousand people who liked that tweet, but to me, a 50 percent chance of doing nothing and my life being ruined feels pretty risky to me. I don't know that it's wrong though. Oftentimes, when all the choices seem bad, doing nothing presents itself as the best option. But is it?

In addition, people are bad at calculating risk in their daily lives. You are probably taking risks right now that you don't fully understand or didn't consider. There isn't any option that doesn't carry some risk.

Investing is risky; not investing is also risky. Bitcoin is risky; not exploring new ways to grow your income is also risky. Saving money is challenging; so is going broke. There is no financial state that someone exists in that doesn't have its challenges and risks. Education decisions for your kids are risky. With public school education, you risk being at the mercy of whatever school district you live in. With private school education, you risk your kid(s) growing up entitled. With homeschool education, you risk your kid(s) growing up socially awkward. It's all risky. What you are looking for to go to the next level in your life is not the safest option, but one that you can actually enjoy.

Every mode we live in, we find our safe zone. We build a framework for decision-making that makes us feel like we control risk so we can get comfortable. Many of our ideas about comfort and safety come from somewhere—probably our parents or cultures—but we need to learn to see beyond what is "acceptable" risk and gauge risk for ourselves.

I would argue that, in this day and age, following a conventional path to success is actually very risky. Very few jobs are stable enough or pay well enough to guarantee the house, the car, the long-lasting partnership, the college education, the kids, and the vacations we all thought were coming to us. We cannot avoid change, and we cannot do nothing. Life is risky, so we might as well take the risks that will help us reach our potential.

HOW TO EMBRACE THE FAILURE THAT COMES WITH TAKING RISKS

There are many kinds of risks you can take. Having built a career on the subject of failure, I have experienced quite a few. Dumb risks, calculated risks, low risks, high risks—there are lots of ways to shake up your routine and put yourself out there. If you feel stuck or bored, this chapter will help bring movement to your life.

The great thing about risk is that it is a lot less mystical than self-awareness or self-improvement. There are practical ways you can begin assessing and taking life-changing risks. If you are someone who has been in a rut for a while or is naturally change-averse, you can start off slow.

1. Remain a Student of the Future

I am in the content creation business, and I do this every day. I am in a constant cycle of content creation and content curation, which are different but can intersect based on our goals for the content. The number of skills I have had to pick up—video editing, video production, distilling profound thoughts into 280 characters—will only continue to grow. Because the future requires something of all of us, right? We have to continue positioning ourselves as students of what's in store.

If people had to describe your skills and passions, what would they say? Of course, you want to build expertise, but you don't want to be the person who is only good at Photoshop. When no one needs Photoshop anymore because apps have made design attainable for the average user or become cheap to outsource to other geographies, what happens to you?

We all know people who are regularly trying new things, traveling to new places, and experimenting with hobbies. You may not have the luxury of some of these activities, but the only person who is limiting your ability to learn is you. We all have the internet at our fingertips. There is no excuse to limit yourself to one lane and stick to it.

What have you always been curious about? How can you learn more? Do you need to take a class? Get a degree? Buy a skateboard? Learn to code? Masterclass has a paid subscription to learn from the best, but there is also YouTube, where you can learn just about anything in the world for free—if you don't mind the ads. Know this: the adventures you create for yourself keep you unstuck because you're always trying new things.

For example, recently I made the decision to move my primary means of communication with my subscriber outreach from an email subscription to a text message subscription. In the content creation business, conventional wisdom says you need a mailing list where you gather emails and count subscribers and reach out to your people. Mailing lists, from TinyLetter to Mailchimp to Substack (which is just curated email lists and has a $650 million valuation as of this writing), are a giant business. This business model works for a lot of content providers, but I was looking for something new to add to our toolkit.

I looked at the data of the email list I had from engagement to the time it would take my team to create them, and I realized the return on investment was incredibly low. The open rate on our emails was consistently 8 to 11 percent. That was industry standard, but guess what the open rate on text messages is? 97 percent.

So my team and I became students of a new way to engage with our audience through texting. Instead of sending out a regular update email, I give subscribers the choice to opt into a weekly encouraging text through an app called Community. Right now, thousands of people each week receive an encouraging text directly from my phone to theirs. (Text "HEY" to 469-809-1201 to join us.)

The kind of brand we want to have at our company is one that feels a little more personal. The text community I have isn't just a group of people who scroll past the text and move on (they can always unsubscribe). These are people I've connected with over the years through events, services, and social media. They often text me back, and I respond.

This year, I got hundreds of photos of people's Thanksgiving dinners. It blew up my phone, but I loved it. Unlike email, there is no pressure to make the text look good—it's just a text—and it brings me real connection with my audience. I didn't know how it would go when we decided to go for text, but it's creating a level of connection that we didn't previously have with emails.

Is there something new you need to learn to get to the next level? There are many people who choose a lane and stay in it. They provide a really good service, but they don't know how to tell anybody. Or maybe they are a great storyteller with horrible products. The amount of excellent books that were written and forgotten because the authors were terrible at marketing probably numbers in the millions.

Sometimes, to win in your career and life, you have to step beyond your comfort zone and be prepared to wear multiple hats. Sometimes your environment may want you to pick a lane, but is that your definition of success or theirs? You may have to learn a new skill or convince someone who already has that skill to help you.

This applies to our personal lives too. Parenting has changed a lot over the last few decades as have marriage roles. Dating is drastically different than it used to be. (*So I've heard. Been married for a decade now.*) The challenges a middle school student has today are far different from the challenges I had when I was in middle school. In light of what your future requires of you professionally and personally, how are you equipping yourself to bring your best self to the table?

2. Assess Your Risk Affordability

All risks are not created equal. What I can afford to try in terms of my resources could look completely different from yours. I run my own business. You may have a traditional nine-to-five job. But regardless of your career path, you have to consider what risks you can and cannot take.

In the public speaking industry, everyone is supposed to choose their "thing" and devise an entire brand and persona around it. That's "how it's done." From the beginning, I didn't understand it. Everyone assumed I was the "Failure Guy" (a dubious thing to be) because of my documentary and book. But I can talk about many other things besides failure. And what happens when your keynote goes stale? Or people don't want to talk about failure anymore?

I resisted the attempts to fit me into a box. "Tell me the greatest challenges your teams and leaders have, and I'll develop content around that," I would tell clients. It made them uncomfortable at first, but being nimble enough to address any organizational issues—which are all just people issues—broadened my ability to add value by speaking on subjects that helped to relieve organizational pain points. When I began offering subjects beyond failure to my clients, the risk I was taking was their choosing another speaker. Well, my company has enough revenue to sustain one rejection. It does not have enough revenue to sustain ten.

I also have to assess how much of my time and money I want to invest in the different components of my business. I wear multiple hats in multiple lanes between speaking, writing, and coaching. When writing a book, I have to assess what I can and cannot say. I have to assess how informal or formal I want to be when telling a story. My publisher can suggest changes that may be more formal and proper for a reader. At the same time my writing style is more conversational. As a result, I have to find a balance between my education, my experience, and my voice and how I bring those into a book.

There are so many rules regarding what you can and cannot put in a book. But I try to focus on what I can do that is a little bit different. I'm sure there are many rules of what you can and can't do given your schedule or career. But what *can* you do? What don't you need permission to change? Assess that and then make changes.

When gas prices skyrocketed during the first quarter of 2022 in the United States, I remember going to the gas station to fill up my wife's car and realizing we can afford an expensive tank of gas without it impacting our budget significantly, but I know that isn't true for a lot of people. I thought, *I'm willing to bet there's a large number of people who are struggling this week and probably another large number of people who could and would help them.*

Thinking about this, I was getting ready to send out an encouraging message to my text community and decided to try something different.

Instead, I sent a message with a video simply stating that there are often people in our world who have more than enough and people in our world who don't. The text read,

469-809-1201

I woke up this morning wanting to help people who are struggling to afford a tank of gas. So today's text is for two groups of people. 1. Those who need financial help. 2. Those who can afford to help the 1st group. If you're in group 1, help is on the way and simply respond to this text with the number "1". If you're in group 2, respond with the number "2" for further instructions.

My company turned into a bank for twenty-four hours via Venmo, and we raised thousands of dollars to help families in need. We created a small environment for strangers to help some strangers. The stories were incredible. One person texted me back and said their dad had just passed away and they weren't sure how they would pay for gas to get to the memorial.

When I had the idea for the text, some people said, "You can't do that because there will be people who take advantage of the system." I assessed the risk—and the reward of helping a lot of people outweighed the risk of dealing with a few shady people.

Depending on your definition of success, you may have to assess how trying something new might impact the time you get to spend with your family. You might have to assess whether or not the risk you need to take requires getting a new job or simply making it your side hustle. You never want to mistake a hobby for a career. Don't quit your day job without assessing whether or not your household budget can afford it.

Some risks will cause you to take a leap of faith. As a person of faith, I'm all for that. But sometimes you need to take a leap of wisdom. I'm not the person who will tell you to get outside the box just because. No, you need to do as much homework and research as you possibly can to put yourself in a position to succeed. You're going to fail along the way, but it shouldn't be because you didn't assess avoidable challenges.

3. Don't Be Afraid to Look Dumb

I speak around 120 times a year. Most people wouldn't know this, but of those 120 times, 115 of them I try something brand new. I try a joke, change a line, change three lines, test a different story, or speak on totally different topics. I am constantly tweaking my message to see what helps people the most. I'm factoring in current events, time zones, continents, and industry trends as I present new concepts and ideas. Sometimes it works; oftentimes it doesn't.

I have accepted that my keynotes will never be perfect, but they will continue to get better and better if I can always be in the mindset that stepping outside my comfort zone can produce great results. This applies in my personal life as well. If I only did things I was sure my family and friends (often our most honest critics) wouldn't roast me for, I'd never try anything new.

One weekend I tried singing on stage during a message at church. I do not sing—at least, I don't sing well enough to be asked to do so. I wish I could say I started small, but I didn't. I went for "Ain't No Mountain High Enough"—Whitney Houston's rendition, specifically. I was awful—and for some odd reason people loved it.

The top videos on TikTok are people trying things and failing. I don't know why failure gets such a bad rap, considering it is the natural consequence of any serious attempt at growth—and people find it extremely entertaining. Do you want to know what every successful person you admire, read about, or follow has in common? They've all failed. So why not embrace the very thing that made them who they are?

Failing often doesn't mean you're going to fail always. You are looking for that one time you knock it out of the park. You have to try new stuff because you have no idea when that will be. Fear of failure—even as a result of past failure—is a terrible reason to never try. People are bold not because they think they won't fail but because they have assessed failure and assigned its proper weight.

I wish that the fear of looking dumb was a problem we got to leave behind in middle school. It isn't. So many of us are afraid to look stupid. We hold in our questions, stay in our lanes, and never post to the social media accounts we made all because we are afraid of someone judging us.

It isn't just that we don't want people to think we are dumb; we actually want people to think we are experts. We want to do cool stuff and look cool doing it. We want to ski black diamonds in style, not pizza our way down the bunny slopes. For some reason, the latter is embarrassing, even if it's our first time on the mountain. Why is that? Why aren't people willing to be beginners?

We also get locked into a specific vision of ourselves. Just like, "We don't do that," we start thinking, "That's not us" or "That's not me." Who says a great pair of Jordans aren't you? I will often take my executive coaching clients shopping for new clothes or send them fashion choices that are way outside their established norm. I can see the doubt in their eyes. "Just try it!" I tell them.

We all know the person who has had the same haircut for thirty-five years. It probably was outdated back when they got it in 1985—and they're *still* hanging on. The same could be said of a lot of people's jeans. There is a difference between tradition, a grounded sense of self, and getting so stuck in your ways you can't even imagine yourself with bangs. What are we so afraid of?

People spend their entire lives being calculated, but at some point, you need to start moving toward what intimidates you. This is probably your greatest area for growth.

For a lot of people, technology is very intimidating. There's even a term for it: technophobia. Smart phones and tablets and smart devices can be challenging for people who grew up in an analog world. The same is true for athletic feats. How many people dream about running 5Ks or joining a boxing gym but are too afraid to get off the couch? Yeah, you probably will look dumb that first time you hit the gym. But who cares? Until you get over that fear, nothing changes for you.

I am grateful for all the people who were willing to look dumb. Do you realize all of the companies we would have never heard of if people weren't willing to try something new? Do you know what Google's original name was? BackRub.[16] That's right. They changed the name back in 1998. Imagine meeting someone for the first time and saying, "BackRub me." (What?!) But we would never have Google if someone wasn't willing to start with BackRub.

Blue Ribbon Sports sounds like a decent name for a company. But Nike has a much better ring to it. Back in 1893, there was a guy named Caleb Bradham who was a pharmacist experimenting with a few different soft drink recipes. He created a mix of sugar, water, caramel, lemon oil, nutmeg, and other natural additives that people loved. But five years later, Brad's Drink was renamed Pepsi-Cola. Subway used to be called Pete's Super Submarines. And eBay used to be called AuctionWeb.

What does this mean for you? It means you shouldn't despise a humble or dumb beginning. My life is a lot better because of people who decided to get off the beaten path and risk society's judgments.

LIFE POST-FAILURE

When you take risks, sometimes you will fail. How badly you fail will depend on the magnitude of the risk you took, which is something you should assess before you dive in headfirst. In fact, you should write down your worst-case scenario. If it looks survivable, then what is holding you back from taking a chance on things turning out well?

In my coaching practice, I am surprised by how much pressure people put on decisions without figuring out what the real damage could be. Why are the stakes always so high? A realistic assessment of risk requires clear sight but also a calm mind and a reluctance to indulge in hyperbole. "This person could tank our business," a client might tell me. But could they really? If not, what is the true fear?

Sometimes the failure wasn't in our idea but in the execution. While you don't want to bread crumb your mistakes or failures, you do want to figure out what went wrong. Did you miscalculate the risk? Or did you just do a poor job making it happen? Was there a critical skill set you lacked? How are you going to do things differently in the future?

Usually, the biggest risks we take that burn us are the ones we take on other people. However, we cannot let one bad experience with someone kill our ability to take risks on people forever. This is a little bit like making choices from bad data. People are going to disappoint you. But they are also going to amaze you! The horror stories we like to tell about trusting people who did not work out should not define our narratives or stop us from showing up for others.

You've likely heard the common expression, "Fool me once, shame on you. Fool me twice, shame on me." But is it really only two strikes now? If I only had two chances, I would not be where I am today. So many people took chances on me even when I didn't perform at my best or make the best choices.

Last year, I did a virtual event for a giant company for an hour—and my audio was off the entire time. It was just my face talking at them with no sounds coming out, like the world's most energetic silent movie. The client was trying to get my attention in the chat to let me know something was wrong, but my slides were full screen and I never saw their messages. The only thing I could do was apologize profusely.

Thank goodness they gave me another chance, and I was given the opportunity to speak in front of a few of their divisions. They took a risk by bringing back the guy who didn't triple-check his audio jack, and I appreciated the second chance extended to me.

Your willingness to take risks on people should extend from your professional life to your personal life. While our ambitions should feature prominently in our lives, there are times when we need to support someone else's dream. We need to take a risk on their startup, their budding influencer career, or their writing, and support them. Because people are human, we also need to prepare to be let down personally and professionally. Ultimately though, you will regret the times you chose not to support someone more than the times you did.

A quote often misattributed to Mark Twain states, "Twenty years from now you will be more disappointed by the things you didn't do than by the ones you did. So, throw off the bowlines, sail away from the safe harbor, catch the trade winds in your sails. Explore. Dream. Discover."[17]

I encourage you this week to simply try something new and be willing to learn from the results. Because I believe you're only failing if you're failing to learn from your failures.

CHAPTER RECAP

- The world has and will continue to change. Will we?
- We can't go to the next level in our professional or personal life without taking some sort of risk.
- To embrace risk, we also have to be willing to chase failure, whether that means becoming a student of the future or not being afraid to look dumb.
- There could be someone in your life whom you need to take a chance on.

DO THIS NOW

Whether it's a hobby, a food, or a new skill, go try something new this week!

CHAPTER 7

THE ASSIST QUESTION

Whose dream do I need to support?

You can have everything you want in life
if you just help enough people.
—Zig Ziglar

What do Andre Walker, Josh Lipton, Jon Favreau, Lis Lewis, Steve Williams, Brandon Payne, Chris Castaldi, Susan Batson, Scott Feeley, Jim Berger, Tina Knowles, and Regunatha Pichai have in common?

First, you've probably never heard of most of them.

Second, they each played a supporting but critical role in helping someone else's dream happen.

Andre Walker is a hairstylist who has won seven Daytime Emmy Awards for Outstanding Achievement in Hairstyling for his work on *The Oprah Winfrey Show*.[1] Josh Lipton was considered to be Steve Jobs's right-hand man.[2] Jon Favreau was Barack Obama's speechwriter during his first term.[3] Lis Lewis is a vocal coach whose clients have included Miguel, Gwen Stefani, Rihanna, Courtney Love, Britney Spears, Colbie Caillat, Linkin Park, Demi Lovato, Iggy Azalea, and Jack Black.[4]

Steve Williams was Tiger Woods's caddie for thirteen of his first fourteen majors wins.[5] Brandon Payne is Steph Curry's personal trainer.[6] Chris Castaldi is the assistant film director for

Avengers: Endgame, Avengers: Infinity War, Jurassic World, Captain America: Civil War, Transformers: Revenge of the Fallen, Iron Man, Iron Man 2, and *The Chronicles of Narnia: The Lion, the Witch and the Wardrobe* (just to name a few).[7]

Susan Batson is an acting coach who has enjoyed the privilege of working with Nicole Kidman, Tom Cruise, Jennifer Lopez, Chris Rock, Jamie Foxx, Sean "Diddy" Combs, Liv Tyler, Jennifer Connelly, and countless other actors searching for truthful connections between themselves and the characters that they play.[8] Scott Feeley and Jim Berger were the producers behind Chip and Joanna Gaines's *Fixer Upper.*[9]

Tina Knowles, born Celestine Ann Beyoncé, is the mother of Beyoncé, the one you've definitely heard of.[10] From encouraging her daughter throughout childhood to follow her dreams, to becoming the stylist for Destiny's Child, Beyonce's all-female singing group from the '90s and 2000s, Tina put her daughter first. Regunatha Pichai, father of Google CEO Sundar Pichai, spent the equivalent of a year's salary on Sundar's plane ticket to the United States so he could attend Stanford.[11]

They're all unsung heroes of other people's dreams.

As a motivational speaker, I used to believe my job was to inspire and equip people to take steps toward *their* dreams. That is until I did an event in Phoenix, where, during a Q&A session with the audience, someone stood up in the audience and asked, "What do I do if I don't really have a dream?"

In that moment, I realized that every message I'd listened to, every podcast I'd put on, and every book I'd read was filtered through the lens of, *How does this help me achieve my goals, my dreams, and my pursuit of GOATness and my definition of success?* But here was an executive who was trying to figure out what to do with all the practical steps and motivational stories I had just shared.

That's when it dawned on me. I can't just be someone who

equips people to achieve their dreams. I also need to be someone who equips people to help *others* achieve their dreams. Sometimes in the process of trying to make history we lose sight of what's important in the present.

Whenever you find yourself stuck at one level in your life, one of the things you can do is look for someone else who's also stuck and help them get to the next level.

When venturing into helping someone else, we think we have to have the proper credentials to help them. We certainly don't want to overstep boundaries, but helping someone else go to the next level may not require having more experience or education than they have. Sometimes it just requires a perspective they don't have.

Looking at the size of the companies on my client roster, my business is significantly smaller than theirs. So what could I bring to the table that would help them level up? One of the things I have that no one else in their organization does is an outside perspective. I am able to ask them objective questions and equip them to walk away from our conversation with some clarity.

We all have people in our homes and careers with goals and dreams. We are in their lives for a reason. Imagine the type of person you would become and the growth you'd experience if the people in your life felt like you supported their dreams. As the esteemed Maya Angelou says, "Be a rainbow in somebody else's cloud."[12]

DREAM DETECTIVES

It is easy to become the center of our own universe. It is easy to think that our lives are about our success, our incomes, our homes, our cars, our education, our love lives, and our careers. We can start believing that everyone exists in our world to help us improve our stuff. I think this mindset is reflected in how we discuss self-development.

For example, consider this phrase we have all adopted over the years: "Surround yourself with good people." The premise is fine, but the sentence implies that *you* are at the center of your friendship circle. Everyone is in your orbit, and if you get to choose who surrounds you (lucky), the assumption is that *you* are a good person who deserves to also have good people supporting you.

Taken from another angle, though, you are no longer in the center. When someone else thinks of the people surrounding them, that might include you. If we are all the sum of the five people we spend the most time with, you are one of someone else's five. You are surrounding someone else. We can't exist as someone who is only in relationships to be served. Relationships should be a two-way street. You help me grow, and I should help you grow.

One of my favorite stories is about the relationship expert and bestselling author Dr. John Gottman. One day he was sitting with his publisher, trying to convince them to increase the marketing budget for his book *The Seven Principles for Making Marriage Work*.[13]

The meeting was not going well. Dr. Gottman could tell the head of marketing was skeptical. Finally, the man spoke up. "Look, in thirty seconds, tell me the one thing I can do to improve my marriage."

Dr. Gottman thought about it. "Well," he said, "the book has a lot of really great advice in it, but if I had to pick one, it would be to honor your wife's dreams."

The guy stood up and walked out of the room.

That didn't go very well, Dr. Gottman thought to himself.

But the marketing executive hadn't walked from the meeting because he was over it. Here is what Dr. Gottman learned later:

The man had been stunned. He and his wife had been married for a long time. He loved her, but he had no clue what *her* dreams were. So, he left the office, got on the subway, and showed up unannounced at their Brooklyn home.

"Did you get fired?" his concerned wife asked.

"No," he told her. "But I had this guy in the office and . . . I was wondering, what are your dreams?"

She looked right at him. "I thought you'd never ask."

When we see people every day, we get in the habit of believing we know everything about them. The daily minutiae of all the administrative aspects of life can overtake the deep conversations we might have had when we first met them. What we need to become, Dr. Gottman advises, are dream detectives.[14]

Our mandate is to discover the dreams of the people closest to us. What does your partner dream of? Your kids? Your favorite coworker? Your boss? Your parents? Your roommate? Your best friend? What are their goals? What are their definitions of success and how can you help them succeed? People might not always have a clear answer, but the benefit of being able to see them one step removed means that you can be their sounding board. Reflect back at them their desires, interests, and how they spend their time. You can give them the gift of clarity with love.

When I say your family needs support, I do not mean just financially. Sometimes the breadwinner's favorite card to play is, "I put a roof over your head, I pay the bills around here, I paid for your school, and I gave you a car." It is as if financial support exonerates them from providing emotional support. As a person of faith, I think spiritual support for my family is just as important as financial support.

More and more I am learning the value of presence over presents. I provide for my family, but what the people close to me want most is my authentic undivided attention. For me to be in the room with my phone put away and my focus on them. The best way I can assist others is often with my time.

Before you go looking for people to support, make sure you check in with the people closest to you. This is your inner circle. Only when those people's needs are attended to (and there will be plenty of them) should you turn your gaze outward. You do not want to help people you don't know at the expense of people you do.

Ask yourself, Do the people in my life feel supported in their dreams?

Does my partner/spouse feel supported?

Do my children feel supported?

Does my family feel supported?

Do my friends feel supported?

Then you can ask, Is there somebody else who also needs my help to follow their dreams and reach their goals?

THE COST OF A CUP OF COFFEE

Did you know that Starbucks almost wasn't the green, Venti behemoth that it is today? If it hadn't been for Bill Gates Sr.—that's right, Microsoft's Bill Gates's dad—Starbucks as we know it might never have existed.

Way back in 1987, a young entrepreneur named Howard Schultz was running a coffee company, Il Giornale coffeehouses.[15] He heard Starbucks, then only six stores, was coming up for sale for $3.8 million. His dream was running the business, which he had briefly been a part of for a few years before starting his own. He was given ninety days to raise the money to purchase.

Two months into fundraising, Schultz got a call that another business titan in town was outbidding him by putting in an all-cash offer for $4 million. Schultz's attorney told him the senior partner at his firm might be able to help and set up a meeting for young Howard.

Schultz didn't know who his lawyer's senior partner was, but he came in and found out it was indeed Bill Gates Sr. What most people underestimate about Bill Gates Sr. is not his wealth, but his height. He's six-foot-seven! As intimidating as Gates could be, Gates heard Schultz out and then told him they were going for a walk. Schultz was petrified.

Without saying another word, Gates and Schultz began walking to the office of the titan who was trying to make his own deal with Starbucks.

"You should be ashamed of yourself that you're going to steal this kid's dream. It's not going to happen. You and I both know this is not going to happen," Gates told the guy.

And that was that.

What Bill Gates Sr. did was leverage every inch of his six-foot-seven frame and influence to help a young entrepreneur have an opportunity to go for his dream. That's how Howard Schultz became the CEO of Starbucks and turned it into a global phenomenon. What if you could use your influence, big or small, to do something similar for someone else?

There are three ways I believe the people in your personal and professional life can be supported by you:

1. Support others with your influence.

Someone I've seen take this to a new level is TikTok star Jimmy Darts (@jimmydarts if you want to follow), who creates content that has been described as "stunts of kindness." In his viral videos, he's seen walking up to random people and looking for a way to make their day. He's given strangers a variety of things like flowers, toys, cash, and even cars![16]

In some cases, he'll actually ask the stranger for something small—for example, in one video he asked a guy sitting outside of a donut shop if he had any spare change to help him get a donut. The guy agreed, but when he reached in his pocket, he realized he didn't have any money. So instead of buying Jimmy a donut, the guy offered him a piece of his own. Jimmy responded by giving this stranger $500 to thank him for his kindness.

One time Jimmy's challenge was asking a family with kids to buy him a gallon of milk and if they did, he would respond by giving them $10,000. In the video, the family hands him a couple bucks to get the gallon of milk and he responds by telling them they can fill up their cart with as much stuff as they want for Christmas.[17]

A family that was trying to figure out their own budget was kind enough to help someone else get a gallon of milk. When they got to the parking lot to put everything in the back of their truck, they were handed $10,000 in cash.

Jimmy has partnered with organizations, car dealerships, and his millions of followers to spread kindness and, in some cases, help get people off the street through crowdfunding. Jimmy encountered a man experiencing homelessness named Tom, who had a sign that read, "Will work any jobs day or nite $5.00 per hour."[18]

Jimmy said he wanted to help but realized Tom needed a friend first. He asked Tom what was on his bucket list, and he said, "Hitting some baseballs." So Jimmy took him to play baseball. Then he took him to Disneyland and Chick-fil-A. Jimmy invited his followers to raise money to help get Tom off the streets.

One of the hurdles Tom had in getting a job was he only had three teeth, but by leveraging his social media platform, Jimmy was able to raise enough money to get Tom a brand-new smile, some clothes, a haircut, a place to stay—and then Tom was offered a job all because Jimmy used his influence to help a stranger who became a friend.

You may not have the social following of Jimmy Darts or the money and clout that Bill Gates Sr. or Jr. have. But you do have a level of influence that can help someone whom you may be underestimating. There is so much power in a suggestion or recommendation, whether it is putting two people together for coffee or throwing someone's name in the hat for a new role.

One of our team members, Lacey Stenson, is the queen of making recommendations and connections. When I started my podcast, I had no idea what I was doing, but Lacey leveraged her network and made over thirty introductions between myself and highly influential people in her sphere of influence. She could and should write her own book and do her own thing, but she'd rather spend her time, energy, and resources to help other people like myself accomplish their goals.

Many times when a job has opened up with one of my clients, I've seen a middle manager say, "I have two people you should consider. They are slightly underqualified, but they could be worth giving a chance to." There's at least one person in your life whom you can use your voice or platform to help. Sometimes it's a teammate who doesn't get playing time. Sometimes it's a barber trying to build clientele. Sometimes it's a local restaurant that a lot of people haven't heard about. Sometimes it's a colleague who can't catch a break.

That little nudge is all that is needed for someone to land a dream job or significantly boost their career. Everyone is asking, "What does this do for me?" when we could be asking, "What can I do for them?" "You can go to work and actually make someone else's job less miserable," writes Patrick Lencioni, bestselling author of *The Five Dysfunctions of a Team*. "Use your job to help others."[19]

I have to be careful when I do this, but I love telling my clients about the creatives who work on my team. I know I run the risk of them being stolen, but they're not my property. I want them to get more business outside of ours and grow in their own lane. Ultimately, I think we have to look inside our sphere of influence and begin to think through if there's anybody who could use an assist from us via recommendation, suggestion, or connection.

2. Support others by exposing them to new opportunities.

Sometimes leveraging your influence for others is through exposure. People often need to see it before they can be it, but they haven't been in the right rooms to know what success even looks like.

I was speaking to a group of travel agents recently about diversity, equity, and inclusion (DEI). One of them asked me, "Why does our industry lean so *white*? And what can I do about that?"

I'm not a travel agent, so I really didn't know if that was true or why that might be the case. However, I did take a guess.

I explained to her that, in the lower-income community I grew up in that was predominantly full of people of color, there was a fairly narrow definition of success. You could play professional sports, or you could get into music and entertainment.

Nobody in my neighborhood was considering being an accountant or computer programmer or lawyer or dentist or *travel agent*. I am not saying people I grew up with weren't capable of thriving in any one of those professions. It's just that I didn't know any high-profile Black travel agents growing up. I didn't even know it was an option. I simply did not have that exposure.

My advice to the travel agent that day? Start looking for opportunities in her city to create exposure in neighborhoods that weren't aware of how her business worked.

One of my clients is in data solutions. When I first started working with them, they were humbly asking good questions about how they could make an impact for their clients and their community. Over the course of a year, they started hosting math and science fairs at schools in lower-income neighborhoods. They then offered scholarships for students interested in getting degrees in that particular field to create career pathways for students in fields they had previously not been exposed to.

Because I went to a private school growing up, I had the opportunity to spend time across town with a friend whose father was a senator and business owner. He taught me a lot about finances, investments, and running a business. He exposed me to a whole new way of living. The impact that transfer of knowledge made on my life was tremendous.

Whether it is your office or your home, you cannot make the mistake of underestimating the influence you have on each person who walks in and out of your environment. Maybe there is a birthday party happening at your house. The way you host and treat people could be showing someone at that party what a hospitable home looks like.

Your impact could be showing people what a healthy, loving marriage looks like. Some people never want to get married because they've never seen a good one. Some people struggle with parenting because they weren't parented very well. Sometimes the best way you can support others is by giving them a front-row seat to something they wouldn't have seen without you.

3. Support others with your time.

Los Angeles Rams offensive tackle Andrew Whitworth won the 2021 Walter Payton NFL Man of the Year award. That award is presented annually by the NFL to honor a player's volunteer and charity work as well as his excellence on the field. Upon receiving the award, Andrew delivered a speech that moved the crowd at SoFi

Stadium and those watching on TV, calling upon those listening to invest time in their communities. During his speech he told a story that challenged me. Here's what he said:

> Going on school visits, providing STEM labs, hospital visits, programs for military, or just going to local food banks and helping out with homeless shelters, all of those have been amazing. But one experience brought it all together for me. This year. And it happened on a football field. In our game against the Detroit Lions, I had a young player from the Lions run up to me as soon as the final horn went off. And I saw him sprinting over and I didn't know what was going on. Like we'd known each other forever. I couldn't place him. It made me so nervous. Had I actually played long enough that a coach's son or player's son is playing against me?
>
> The young player then said, "Hey, man. You're not gonna remember me. I'm Derrick Barnes. You spent time with me when you were a young player in Cincinnati at the Boys and Girls Club. And it meant the world to me. You used to sit with me and talk to me about life and I was just a little kid. I wanted you to know how much it meant to me. You know what? The main thing I wanted to say, Whit, I made it. I made it to the NFL, Big Whit."[20]

He concluded his speech encouraging his other NFL comrades, saying, "On that Tuesday off day, what every guy who's sitting in this room that's played knows, I'd rather be at home. I made an investment in him. And I didn't even know it. I think that's a great lesson for all of us. None of us know when the moment's gonna present itself. The key is to always be available when it does."

One of the ways we can assist others is with our time. When someone takes the time to show their support of something or someone we care about, doesn't it mean the world to us? I have plenty of friends who've purchased my books. I feel very supported by that. But I've also had a few friends who purchased the book and actually took the time to read it and then took the time to tell me their favorite part. (Some tell me what I should have done better.)

Don't we all have someone in our world trying to get something off the ground? It could be a podcast or a YouTube channel or a business or a blog. What if you took some time today and just showed your support? Like. Retweet. Share. Subscribe. Listen. Comment. Be the person you wish you had in your life supporting you. Assist somebody you know and love. Volunteer at a non-profit and sit with somebody like Andrew Whitworth did for Derrick Barnes.

I have a friend who was at the beginning of his journey of creating digital content. As we talked about in the previous chapter on risk, I encouraged him to step outside of his comfort zone and try some new things. He sent me some stuff he wrote, and I told him I thought it would be received better via video.

My friend wasn't an in-front-of-a-camera type of guy, but he tried it anyway. All he asked of me was to take time to give him feedback on the videos. The first one wasn't great, but it was better than him doing nothing. I called him and gave him seven or eight tweaks he could make for future videos. What I realized was all my friend really needed from me was a little bit of my time.

Whether it's our spouse, boss, children, or neighbor, it means something when we take time to let them know we've got their back.

Operating this way is one method to ensure you are a difficult person to lose. If you're a person who is constantly supporting others and looking for ways to add value to the room, why would any company fire you? If your family consistently feels supported by you, why wouldn't they want to be around you?

I filter every meeting I sit in, every speech I give, and every coaching session I run by looking for ways to support somebody else's dream. Sometimes this means using my voice to ask the unaskable question. Sometimes this means listening because I already have a voice.

Becoming someone who supports others is not easy. At first, you might even find it overrated. People aren't always grateful or don't always utilize the opportunities you give them like you want them to. But when you have a twenty-year track record of helping other people, it will change your life in the process of helping theirs.

There's an old Chinese proverb that goes like this:

> If you want happiness for an hour, take a nap.
> If you want happiness for a day, go fishing.
> If you want happiness for a year, inherit a fortune.
> If you want happiness for a lifetime, help somebody.[21]

When you're thinking about your endgame and your definition of success, I hope that definition includes helping someone else succeed. Next-level people figure out ways to make room for other people's perspectives, experiences, and, most importantly, dreams. The feeling you get from watching others win with your support will far surpass any goal you make yourself.

CHAPTER RECAP

- Behind every GOAT is someone who seriously supported that person's dream.
- We owe it to our loved ones to become their dream detectives.
- Support people with your influence.
- Support people by exposing them to new opportunities.
- Support people with your time.

DO THIS NOW

Go like, retweet, share, subscribe, listen, comment, or support somebody you care about. Be the person you wish you had in your life supporting you.

CHAPTER 8

THE INTEGRITY QUESTION

What is the right thing to do?

It takes twenty years to build a reputation and five minutes to ruin it. If you think about that, you'll do things differently.
—Warren Buffett

Tax fraud.

Paying someone to do your homework.

Using a fake vaccination card.

Flirting to get ahead.

Cheating on an exam.

Getting someone you don't like fired.

Not hiring someone because of their gender or race.

Lying to your boss.

Stealing a pack of gum.

Charging a customer more than you should.

Cheating on your partner.

Dealing in insider trading.

Fudging sales numbers.

Expensing personal purchases on the company card.

Haven't we all seen a story, a headline, or a documentary about somebody who wrecked their life, career, team, company, or their marriage because they found themselves involved in one of the above activities?

What's interesting about people who intentionally do something even though they know it is wrong is that it's not about right and wrong for them; it's about not getting caught. According to one study on married couples, 74 percent of men and 68 percent of women admit they'd cheat if it was guaranteed they'd never get caught.[1] How many people would steal if they knew they wouldn't get caught? How many people would lie?

Each and every one of us has a moment in our lives where we have the opportunity to do the right thing but are tempted to do the wrong thing, especially if we can get away with it. Let's say you did the crime but didn't have to do the time because you were good at covering your tracks. Is that a win?

The only problem is, don't we know when someone *else* is acting without integrity? We may not always have proof, but we can feel it.

Think about a time someone lied to you and you couldn't prove it. You may not have known what the real story was, but you knew that you weren't getting it. You can feel something's off even if you can't quite put your finger on it. Perhaps you've purchased a vehicle, and while they're telling you that you're getting a deal, you feel like they're robbing you.

A partner can't always prove when the person he or she loves is cheating. But the partner can often sense it. We can feel when something isn't right with others, but do we have the same powers to feel it within ourselves? We can clearly identify the lack of integrity in others but tend to rationalize our own lack of integrity. We have legit reasons to cut corners, and *they* don't.

You and I are tempted to lie primarily because it serves as a self-preservation weapon. It allows us to sell people on the story we want them to believe even though we know it's not true. As much as we'd love to lie to protect ourselves, we loathe being lied to.

I saw an amazing tweet the other day: "I'm not mad you lied to me. I'm mad that I can't trust you anymore," which apparently is paraphrasing Nietzsche. You may have read that quote and thought, *Yes!* Immediately someone came to mind where you felt that about them. But let's just say that person is reading this book too. Are you sure that person has never felt the same way about you?

A lot of people I coach have found themselves making incredibly difficult decisions over the last couple of years. Some of those decisions included whether they could actually get away with getting more money from the government than they needed through the government's Paycheck Protection Program (PPP). All they had to do was check a few boxes that weren't true and all of it would be filed under "COVID Relief."

People had to make decisions about whether to fire, furlough, or keep their full-time employees and hope for the best. There were decisions about whether to open their place of business after the two weeks when we were all supposed to stay home. (That was a long two weeks.)

They had to make decisions about who they would or would not let in their homes, or who they would choose to hang out with, and whether or not it would be indoors or outdoors. They had to make decisions about working from home or working at the office. And sometimes the choice was made for them, whether they liked it or not.

During this challenging time, the integrity question is what I used the most to help coach people when making tough decisions. Because here's what I know about you and me: in our homes and our jobs, if we're asking what the right thing to do is, the people we work with and love will feel it.

This is not the chapter that is going to help you get it right. That's debatable. But the people we care about the most should always know that we're at least *trying* to get it right.

Because asking, "What is the right thing to do?" is going to get you more respect than asking, "What's the most money we can make?" When given the opportunity to do the right thing, I think the people in our worlds need to see us choose that—even if it means we don't get ahead. Because if you have to do the wrong thing to grow the company, you've failed to grow yourself in the process.

WHAT YOU LOSE WHEN YOU LIE

"Whoever is careless with the truth in small matters cannot be trusted with important matters," said the smartest man ever, Albert Einstein.[2]

COVID-19 was a huge litmus test for integrity in corporate America. While corporations' mettle was tested in the alignment between their public messaging and actual execution, working from home also became the litmus for the American workforce. It was not hard to sit on Zoom, Slack, or email . . . and watch movies all day. People stopped asking, "How can I contribute?" and started asking, "What can I get away with?"

The tragedy isn't that people got away with playing video games or interviewing for other jobs while they were supposed to be working. The tragedy is that they may have gotten away with their behavior, but deep down people trust them less because they could tell that person was giving the bare minimum. They might not know their colleagues have lost respect for them, but the shift is there.

When I first began working with larger companies, I was shocked by the number of internal affairs investigations that go on. I have worked with so many organizations where employees were let go and they had no idea why. It was because their boss found out about some egregious behavior and, instead of confronting them, fired them and chalked it up to something else: company restructuring. (Every leader gets creative when it comes to explaining the disappearance of former employees.) The person who was let go may never know the real reason for their termination. But some of the people who are still there certainly do.

It's kind of like gossip. Whenever someone is speaking ill of someone else behind their back, there's a little bit in us that's thinking: *I wonder if this is how they talk about me when I'm not around.* And then what happens? We speak differently around that person because we don't trust them.

When you lie, you lose trust. Trust is very difficult to gain and very easy to lose. It's one thing to lose a job over a lie. It's another thing to lose family or a friend. If you want to level up in your life and your career, you have to level up in building trust with the people you live and work with. To accomplish that, you have to live with a high level of integrity. Because acting without integrity not only harms your relationships with others but it also impacts your relationship with yourself.

LYING IS TRICKING YOURSELF

The basic idea of being a person of integrity is being a person who is whole. What you see is what you get. Who you say you are is someone who can be counted on and trusted. Who you are in public often matches who you are in private. Who you are when no one is watching aligns with who you are when the spotlight is on you.

Losing our integrity is what happens when there is something we really, really want, but we need to bend the rules a little to get it.

What would you be willing to sacrifice your integrity for? The answer probably isn't immediately clear, but there are common weaknesses I see people succumb to all the time. I am not immune, but it breaks my heart to see what people sell out for.

The things people are willing to sacrifice their integrity for include money, applause, love, and power.

Ask yourself:

What have I done for money?

What have I done for applause (including likes, views, and comments)?

What have I done for love?

What have I done for power?

The problem is, whatever money, applause, love, or power you got by lying, you must ask yourself: is it real? If you get a thousand "likes" on Instagram but you bought seven hundred followers, what does that mean? It's not exactly wrong, but is it right?

This is the problem with lying. You may think, *I'm going to get ahead.* But you're not. You *think* you are. You have tricked yourself. The lie is, in and of itself, a lie. You have tricked yourself into believing you got ahead when really, you are losing.

It may not happen today. It might not even happen tomorrow. But if you make a habit of lying, if you tell a particularly egregious lie, or if you lie to the wrong person, it will catch up with you. People might never tell you, but they will slowly stop answering your calls. They may stop doing business with you. They might stop being your friend. They may just go the other direction, and you'll never know what happened.

LOOKING BACK OVER YOUR SHOULDER

Living without integrity has a cumulative effect on your life. Think back to the biggest lie you told as a kid. (Honest answers only—I won't know, and none of us is perfect.) Did anyone ever find out?

Did you spend all your time desperately afraid that someone would catch you? If no one ever did, how long did the fear of being found out follow you?

Unfortunately, we might get more comfortable lying as we enter adulthood. We call it "bending the rules" or justifying our choices. After all, we deserve it. Our actions weren't really that bad. The rules weren't fair to begin with. The speed limit was too low.

Sometimes we get in a "screw the man!" kind of attitude. Taxes are the best example. No one feels like they need to be fair to the IRS. The rules are complicated. The guidelines change frequently. It's somewhat of a guessing game at the beginning of the year for most people hoping their accountant or H&R Block estimates a refund instead of their owing the government a pretty penny. I know of very few tax evaders. But tax fudgers? Well, yeah, I know quite a few. Tax fudgers are the people who cheat in very small ways on their taxes, reducing their taxable income.

According to a survey by Pew Research, 79 percent of people believe cheating on your taxes is wrong. Problem is, the IRS says that 75 percent of people do.[3] Guess what happens when you short-change the IRS? You become *afraid* of the IRS. The IRS didn't need to have that power over you, but now you are hiding something. If they catch you, there could be consequences, the severity of which will depend on what you did. Don't get me wrong—I'm all for a tax write-off. But I've been encouraged at times to look for tax loopholes. *Loophole* is where something just feels off. When we pay our taxes, I don't spend a moment of my life worrying about the IRS. I am never going to get a letter that says I cheated. At the very worst, I might have made a mistake and it will cost money or time to fix, but I am not going to jail for tax evasion or fraud. That seems like a win to me.

Sometimes we ask others to lie for us to cover our tracks. Then, not only are we in on the lie, but someone else also holds our secret. That gives them a power no one should have. It also unfairly puts them in a compromised position. But when we don't have tracks to cover, everyone can go home happy. No one has to worry about the hammer falling.

There is a difference between asking, "What do I have to do to get a leg up on the competition?" (i.e., hitting the gym harder, hiring a trainer, changing your diet) and doing *anything*, including cheating, to win. We've all heard about stories of professional athletes who faked an injury or even dabbled in performance-enhancing drugs because winning meant more than their integrity. Especially with the use of PEDs, they are always looking over their shoulders. The consequences—questionable records, stripped medals, and a ruined reputation—might come years later.

"I don't need to cheat to win," said Serena Williams back in 2018 when a referee accused her of cheating.[4] I think that might be a better attitude to have than "win at all costs." If you cheat, you will likely win. But you won't respect yourself because you'll know what you had to do to make it happen. The pain and agony of living a lie is real. You will feel like a fraud, you will always be looking over your shoulder, and you will lose respect for yourself. You don't want to be in that position.

I was working with a client recently. She is an executive who is high up in a prominent organization in a very competitive industry. (I know; I'm painting a vivid picture.)

"Ryan," she said to me, "how do I uphold my values if my organization has none?"

"What do you mean?" I asked her.

"In our organization, you get ahead by backstabbing, lying, cheating, and inflating the numbers. What should I do?"

I thought about it. Her question really was: "How do I continue to have integrity?"

"How much money do you have saved? 'Cause you should quit," I said.

Just kidding. I did not say that. Remember: we cannot always change our external circumstances, but we can change ourselves. I cannot guarantee you will work for a boss, leader, or organization that always acts with integrity, but that doesn't mean you can't.

Here's what I actually said to her: "You have an opportunity at your job right now to show people how to win *and* do the right thing at the same time. You don't have to choose between being successful or having a good reputation. You can have both. So go crush it and do it with integrity. Show them that you can do what you do at a high level by doing your job with integrity—not having to talk about others behind their backs or lie about your performance to get ahead. Show them that you can get ahead by treating people well and working harder than everybody else."

If you're saying, "I have to cheat to win," then you are saying you are not good enough on your own. Be good enough on your own merit. Be willing to lose rather than winning and compromising your integrity. "Sometimes it is better to lose and do the right thing than to win and do the wrong thing," said Tony Blair in a speech to the House of Commons.[5]

FOUR STEPS TO INTEGRITY

When you are a kid, doing the right thing is presented as a simple choice. Parables and nursery tales usually have a clear-cut moral where the person (or tortoise or mouse) who makes the correct decision is rewarded, and the villain gets theirs in the end. If only real life worked like this.

In our complex, fast-paced, and evolving world, doing the right thing can be simple, but it often isn't. Even if you don't lie, you pay all your taxes, and you never engage in office gossip, you still will occasionally be challenged. Even worse, there may not be a "right" answer. The best you can do is examine your heart, pray on it, and consult trusted advisors.

I can't tell you what the right choice is, but I can offer this framework for helping think through how to act with integrity in a world that doesn't always reward it.

1. Let your good intentions guide you.

A mentor of mine, Ricky Texada, passed away in 2021, but he taught me a tremendous amount about how to live with integrity. His core value was doing the *right* thing for the *right* reason. This means you don't do the right thing for the *wrong* reason, and it also means you don't do things just because you are afraid of getting caught or called out. If doing the right thing will make us look better, any one of us will tend to choose that.

It is interesting to see not just *how* people make decisions but *why* they make them. Good intentions are key on the path to integrity. When faced with a complex decision, first evaluate your own values rather than others' expectations or desires.

This last year we parted ways with an employee at my company. She had received a much better offer elsewhere, and we were happy for her. However, she was leaving right before the holidays. So, the question became, "Should we still give her a Christmas gift?" What was the right thing to do?

To me, it was important that we did right by her, which meant extending a bonus. Even more importantly, I made sure my COO knew we were asking that question and had arrived at an answer. Verbally analyzing the decision-making and inviting other people into the process creates accountability. My other employees understand what I am trying to do and why. For us, we always want to err on the side of generosity because I believe that's the right way to do business.

Intentions are not divorced from impact. You are responsible for both. But, if you can stay centered on improvement ("How can I get better?") and keep your intentions right, you will move toward the right thing. As consultant and writer Peter F. Drucker said, "Doing the right thing is more important than doing the thing right."

2. Ask yourself: What's right for *everyone*?

An important mechanism for shifting your thinking about right and wrong is moving from the question, "What's right for me?" to "What's right for *everyone*?"

Our culture is one of rugged individualism. However, there are real shortcomings to living in a society formulated around extreme individualism. We all live in community with one another, and because of that, our choices and actions have a shared impact, whether we want them to or not.

Living through a pandemic highlighted the whole "living in community" idea and was a revealer of our hearts. Should we open up? Should we shut down? Should we interview for jobs while our bosses have no supervision over us? Should we quit after a week for something better?

For a restaurant during that time, staying closed or opening could be the difference between the business going under or making it. For the owners, the answer was clear: open. But was that the better choice for everyone? Granted, if the restaurant goes under, people lose jobs. So, was there a way to stay open while minimizing health risks to service people and patrons?

If you are asking the right question—how do we serve *everyone*?—you arrive at a much better answer. Sometimes this might mean making less money. Naturally, this is every business leader's great fear—doing the right thing often means sacrificing profits. But that kind of thinking is far too black-and-white and uncreative. It is possible to make plenty of money *and* do right by everyone.

I consider this a lot relative to DEI work. If you are hiring a new employee, one of the foremost questions is what to pay them. What kind of salary can we offer? There are many different factors that can affect that number, but the data shows that demographics are important. Women and people of color are paid, on average, less for the same job even if education and experience are held constant.[6]

Theoretically, you could get away with making a less generous offer and justify it based on many other points—but should you? There is plenty we can call fair if we only make decisions through the prism of what is right for ourselves, but our answers dramatically shift for the better if we can expand our view to encompass the larger circles of our communities.

3. Allow room for multiple choice.

Sometimes we will look at a situation with excellent intentions firmly oriented toward communal good and think, *Huh?*

If the right thing were always obvious, we would probably do a better job of choosing it, even if temptations are high. But we live with a lot of gray space. I don't just mean opportunities to make shady decisions and not get caught, but genuine conundrums that require deep soul-searching and offer myriad possibilities for how we should proceed.

We can all come to different conclusions about what is right, but staying grounded in good intentions and community-thinking is critical. If the people in your world know you are trying to do the right thing, then you will create trust and space for reasonable error.

There is a breakfast spot in Dallas that I love called Snooze. A beloved manager who had worked in the restaurant for years passed away. The day of her memorial, restaurant ownership took the dramatic step of shutting down its location so every employee could attend the service.

Was shutting down the right thing to do? On one level, had they stayed open, they probably would have made tons of money, which would have supported the restaurant and their staff. But how much credibility might they have lost with their employees? And how much loyalty did shutting down earn them?

Shifting away from the applause/love/money/power framework for decision-making, and valuing other things, can help us select the best choice to become who we want to be. Making more money might meet certain goals, but it doesn't automatically make us better people. Earning the loyalty of staff and customers while honoring others certainly does.

4. Invite in accountability.

A homeless shelter reached out to me and told me they had the budget to bring in a speaker. They wanted to know my availability. My COO, who filters all my inquiries, wanted to know how to respond.

Well, first of all, I was not charging a homeless shelter money for me to speak. Why? Because it just felt like the wrong thing to do. Regarding my availability, the best date and time would coordinate with some other projects I may have had going on in the area.

I wanted my COO to know that we were always going to try to do the right thing. Because of this, I hope that if my COO saw me doing the wrong thing, she would call me on it.

Part of walking with integrity is allowing your family, friends, and colleagues to know what you could get away with but decide not to. This isn't done in a self-promoting way. It's done in a way where people can naturally see your character and help you know when you're out of bounds.

Most of us do not have a shortage of opportunities to cheat. Whether you are an intern or the CEO, you can probably get away with a lot. However, your ability to ride out the consequences increases dramatically with your hold on power. Powerful people can often more easily make trouble go away and tend to surround themselves with people who aren't willing or able to be true referees.

The best way to safeguard against the corruption of power is to introduce transparency to your organization or company, inviting others to give feedback. A while back I became interested in *The Great Game of Business*, a theory and book by Jack Stack and Bo Burlingham that pioneered the idea of open-book management. In this model, the entire company has total visibility into organization-wide metrics. This is a bold way to run your business, but it says to your employees, "We have nothing to hide, and you are welcome to ask questions."

This approach can work in your personal life as well. I've got extremely high goals, which, for me, require extremely high accountability and transparency. For example, my wife has my location at all times through the Find My app on our iPhones. My wife's best friend also has my location through the same app. They know where I am 100 percent of the time. There is nothing on my phone my wife can't see. Not that she asks often, but I have nothing to hide. Transparency creates accountability.

I think about the word *confession* often. This is a transparency of intention. What if before you cheated, you told someone trustworthy you were thinking about it? What if before you stole, you confessed to a close friend you were tempted to do so? Having people in your life who can not only help you get better but also act as referees of your less-noble impulses is critical in the journey to integrity.

While you alone are responsible for your choices, having a trusted circle that knows you and can help you make decisions keeps you accountable to the endgame of who you want to be. You may have done some things in your life that were wrong, but it's never too late to start doing the right thing.

On your journey to leveling up, you will be tempted to believe that doing the wrong thing will help you get ahead. What I want you to know is you don't have to do the wrong thing to succeed.

I encourage you to continue to look for the right way to treat your family, friends, and colleagues even when they may not be doing the same. When faced with the opportunity to do the wrong thing that may seem like a shortcut or beneficial for you in the present, choose the right thing. Choose integrity. It may cost you more time and energy in the process, but when you succeed, you'll know you did it with honor.

CHAPTER RECAP

- The people around us can tell when we lie, even if they can't prove it.
- Lying impacts our integrity, even when we think we've gotten away with it.
- Let your good intentions guide you; sometimes you won't get it right, but acting with pure intent matters.
- What's right should be based on more than just what's right for you or what's right financially.
- Sometimes the answer to "What's right?" is multiple choice.
- Transparency always creates accountability.

DO THIS NOW

If it's within your power to right a wrong today, do it.

If you have the opportunity to do the wrong thing today, don't.

CHAPTER 9

THE SCHEDULE QUESTION

How am I managing my time?

*The key is in not spending time, but in investing
it. How will you invest your time this year?*
—Stephen R. Covey

Nine hundred thousand podcasts. That's how many were launched just in the year 2020.[1]

As of January 2022, YouTube has over thirty-seven million channels.[2]

In the self-help category alone, eighty-five thousand books are published a year.[3]

There's about $222.2 billion worth of eLearning courses that we all have access to.[4] We've got more than enough content at our fingertips to help us level up. What we lack is the actual time to apply it all. We've got a surplus of ways to become the best versions of ourselves, but a shortage of margin in our schedules to pull it off.

I remember one time I was sitting with an executive coaching client, and I began to lay out a comprehensive plan to help them develop an internal leadership program.

He responded, "This all looks amazing. I just wish I had time to implement any of it."

Uh oh.

When I started asking other clients and friends about their time, it became clear that most didn't have any extra. This was true whether their jobs (like mine) required travel or they never hopped on an airplane for work. What's the point of consuming all the tips and tools from books, podcasts, videos, and courses if we don't have time to implement our learnings?

I don't think this is just my high-powered executive clients. Everyone struggles with time. The two things people waste most are money and time. Do you know what your spending looks like? Because the average person does not know where their money went last month, whether they're broke or rich. I remember the first time I adopted a budgeting software. I looked at that thing and said, "I spent *how much* on eating out last month?!"

Analyzing my spending was a real wake-up call to create financial goals and a plan to meet those goals. Winging it almost never works. The same is true with time. If you ask most people what they did with their time last month, they probably couldn't tell you. I couldn't, before I began actively auditing my calendar. How much of it did I spend working? Studying? Hanging out with family? Exercising? Watching Netflix? Surfing YouTube? Setting my fantasy basketball lineups?

My, my, my, where did the time go?

When our schedules were disrupted in March 2020, it took us all a few weeks to realize that we were stepping into a new normal that gave most people a large amount of time at home. I've heard, "I finished Netflix" a few times over the last couple of years. That's just how much time people had on their hands.

What I saw then was that in one way or another, people were going to come out of the other side of a pandemic better or worse. I started using this phrase in a lot of my messages, "Don't waste the pandemic." And now I think we have to look back and ask the question, "Did we?"

If we don't take control of our time, someone else will. My iPhone has Screen Time, and it will tell me exactly where my time went. No offense to Netflix, Google, and Apple, but they all have a strategy for how they are going to use my time. I am happy they are being proactive, but I think my plans should supersede theirs.

Just as with money, we should know where our time is going. We should have a time budget that holds us accountable to how we spend our time against our stated goals. Most of us assume we will make time for what's important, but that's not how life works. We have massive goals but a terrible schedule with no margin to actually accomplish those goals.

While the nature of time is theoretical (I'm gonna spare you a meditation on that here), the exercises and tips in this chapter are not. In fact, this may be the most straightforward chapter in the book. Proactively managing your schedule is achievable, even for the busiest among us.

This chapter will help you take your schedule to the next level and learn to maximize your time so what you do is congruent with your mission to accomplish your definition of success.

TIME FLIES—IF WE LET IT

As much as I want to, I cannot create more time. We each only have so much. We are all challenged by a lack of time or a lack of ownership over our time. I don't know anyone who feels like they have enough hours in the day or days in a year.

One of the problems we have with managing our time is that we feel like we don't own it. So much of our time is already spoken for. Our bosses, our kids, our kids' schools, and extracurricular activities pull us in many different directions. Once we have fulfilled all the obligations we have to everyone else, what time can we really call our own? We give time to everyone else without thinking twice. Or, once we get to the limited free time we do have, we are totally exhausted.

Some hyper-organized people are better at tactically managing their schedules, but few people are *intentional* with their time. We do a lot of stuff, but little of it actually impacts our long-term goals. The problem is that life moves fast. If we don't set time toward completing our goals, we will never achieve them.

"One reason so few of us achieve what we truly want is that we never direct our focus; we never concentrate our power. Most people dabble their way through life, never deciding to master anything in particular," says Tony Robbins.[5] I used to envy people who had a full schedule because I equated busyness to success. I used to admire people who worked eighty hours a week until I tried it once. I learned rather quickly just because you have a full schedule doesn't mean it's a good one.

I can look at someone's calendar, and it will tell me pretty quickly the trajectory of that person's career and life. Even if I know nothing else about them, their calendar reveals where they are going by how they spend the majority of their time. So many people tell me their goals and dreams, but their calendar is far from being aligned with them. They want to be an author, but writing isn't anywhere on their schedule. They want to grow in leadership, but they can't show me where leadership development is on their schedule.

Just because we have external limitations placed on our schedules doesn't mean we can't maximize the time we have been given. There's the portion of your schedule outside of your control and then there's the portion of your schedule most definitely in the confines of your control.

We have to start valuing our time, treating it as *the* most valuable and limited resource we have. We need to be very, very careful about how we spend it because we only get so much. Time is money, the old adage goes, an idea that is not theoretical but calculable. Read on to see what I mean.

SEVENTY-NINE YEARS AND COUNTING

Depending on how old you are as you read this book, this next line may encourage or discourage you; nevertheless, it's just math. The average person lives around seventy-nine years.[6] That's 28,835 days if we're numbering them. I hope you get twenty or more years than that, but just in case you're average, you're in that ballpark.

Given those seventy-nine years, the average person will spend twenty-six of those years sleeping. Thirty-three percent of your life you'll be knocked out. And seven years of the seventy-nine, the average person will spend *falling asleep*. So, 2,555 days of your life will be spent tossing, turning, and adjusting pillows to your desired level of sleep comfort. We're already at 41 percent of our lives and we haven't even brushed our teeth yet.

The average person will spend thirteen years working, eleven years looking at screens, and four and a half years eating. At some point, each and every one of us has to come to grips with what we want the years we have on this planet to look like. Your time, your days, your weeks, and your years are extremely valuable. You don't want to waste a minute. A really good friend told me that I should always have one date on the calendar to look forward to. It's some of the best advice I've ever gotten. When looking at your calendar, is there a date on it that you're looking forward to? (More on this in chapter 11.)

The immeasurable things that waste our time include worrying and complaining about things we have no control over. I couldn't find any data about how many years we spend on those things, but my guess would be more years than we eat. Those are years you could be spending energy on your goals and dreams.

Long ago, a mentor of mine sat me down and helped me discover that I was frustrated that other people didn't value my time—only because I didn't value it. That person then taught me to value my time by putting an actual price on it. They had me take my income for the year and divide it by the average number of work hours in a year.

When executives ask how much I charge for an hourly coaching session, I tell them. "That's expensive!" they tell me. But my coaching isn't expensive—my time is. When clients learn about my speaking fee, it's not cheap. But my speaking fee is not just an indication of the value I can bring to an event, it's what I believe is the value of what it costs for me to be away from my family. What I've learned is you cannot expect other people to value your time if you don't.

TIME FOR A CHANGE

When it became clear how time-challenged all my clients are, I realized I had to become a calendar expert. I spent a lot of my own time understanding how people manage their schedules (or don't) and took those hard-earned lessons and applied them to my own life. Strategically and efficiently managing your time is not easy, but the dividends are huge.

People have different strategies for managing their schedules. Some people are "firefighters." Their calendars are dictated by whatever urgent issues crop up in their lives and organizations. They are constantly moving from problem to problem, putting out fires. Their calendars are predominantly reactive.

Other people are "planners." Their time is very tightly controlled and organized. Their days are backed with low margin for error because they are trying to fit in everything. They are the kind of people who are doing everything while accomplishing nothing toward their real long-term goals. They are operationally sound but strategically directionless.

Finally, there are people who manage their time with their endgame in mind. Their calendars are proactive. They decide what is important to them, put that on their calendars first, and then fill in the rest of the gaps with scheduled time for rest too. These people are rare—but this chapter is all about helping you become that type of person.

The first thing I now do with my coaching clients when we begin working together is pull out their calendar. Where are they spending their time? Are they reactive or proactive? Are their activities helping them meet their goals? Welcome to the Calendar Exercise.

This is exactly the exercise I do with my clients, and I want you to do it too.

1

First, pull out your calendar, whether it is digital or paper. Look at the last month. For example, I am writing this in December, so I would open my calendar to November. Then, by percentage, categorize where your time went. It can be harder to quantify entertainment and time with family, but give it a guess and do the math.

Are you surprised by the result? Are you happy with the result?

2

The second part of the calendar exercise is identifying what was unnecessary. Perhaps you had a lot of meetings. What kind? Did you have to attend all of them? What were your biggest time wasters that were within your control? Inevitably, what can you stop doing?

3

The third part of the calendar exercise is identifying what was missing. What's the thing you wish you had done more of professionally or personally? What can you start doing? A lot of leaders spend most of their time putting out fires instead of innovating and building culture. I simply encourage them to put culture-building, innovative items on their calendar.

The point of the exercise isn't to beat you up about your schedule. It's to design an ideal schedule that helps you move toward your actual goals within the confines of what is realistic for you.

I understand not all of your time is yours. How you spend your time can be split into two categories: your *mandated time* and your *free time*. Your mandated time is predetermined. This is time you spend at work, parenting, cleaning, paying bills, or meeting your other basic obligations.

Your free time is everything else. Early in the morning. Your lunch break. Your entire evening until you go to bed. Weekends. How are you using that time? Exercise? Learning new skills? Binge-watching a show? I am betting that before you did this exercise you didn't know. Now you do.

This chapter is going to give you strategies for maximizing both categories. Even your mandated time has wiggle room or can be used more or less effectively depending on where you sit in the hierarchy of your organization. Your free time is totally up to you. You can probably guess what I'm going to say about how you should use it.

(Actually, you might be surprised. Read on.)

FIVE HACKS TO MAXIMIZE YOUR TIME

Hack 1: Schedule Shorter Meetings

If the American workforce were a person, here's what they would say: *I hate meetings.*

I have never met someone who loves meetings, other than a few people who run them, and even they find themselves frustrated. Unfortunately, we can't do business without them. I know some people who went from sitting in meetings at their offices all day to sitting in meetings on Zoom all day.

If you don't have flexibility with your schedule, review my next tip: You have to make peace with being in a lot of meetings and then maximizing your time outside those meetings. If you *do* have flexibility, there are several strategies you can start using right now to unpack your day.

I was sitting with a client of mine who leads a department of forty-plus employees. Her day was truly back-to-back-to-back. It started at 6:30 a.m. and had no breaks until she went home to put her kids to bed. Then, at 9:00 p.m., she was back on email.

Looking at her schedule, I noticed something. "You're the one who sent out all these meeting invites," I pointed out to her.

"Yeah, but I *have* to meet with all these people," she said.

I thought about it. "I guarantee you," I told her, "that everything you have to meet with these people about can be accomplished in forty-five minutes instead of an hour."

She was resistant, but I eventually talked her down to fifty-minute meetings. At least between her meetings, she would have a ten-minute breather to check email, use the restroom, or get a snack. I talk to too many people who get to the end of their day and realize they were so busy they forgot to eat. That is not good.

If someone asks for an hour meeting, offer them forty-five minutes. I know not everyone has this option, but if you do, try it out. It sounds weird, but those fifteen minutes can be a gamechanger.

Trimming the length of your meetings is a gift to other people too. We have all felt people wasting our time, and we hate it. Don't do it to someone else. Acting like your time is valuable and being intentional and efficient with it honors other people's time as well.

I follow this advice myself. I used to coach for an hour for all clients; but now I do thirty minutes for some. How? I cut the fluff. My client and I both know we have thirty minutes, and we maximize the time. At first, it was an experiment. I wasn't sure thirty minutes would be enough to really get into things, but it worked great. Of course, when we are having a genuine conversation and there's nothing coming up on my schedule, the fifteen minutes we add are on me.

Hack 2: Understand Your Prime Time

A poll was done in 2021 by an answering service company, Moneypenny, that asked: Based on the days you work, per week, what day are you most productive?[7] Based on your answer to the previous question, what time of day are you most productive? The poll found that Monday morning at 10:54 a.m. is the time of day Americans say they're the most productive.

For years, science studies have shown that learning is most effective when the brain is in acquisition mode, generally between 10:00 a.m. to 2:00 p.m. and then again from 4:00 p.m. to 10:00 p.m.[8] What this means for you and me is that we have to be mindful of what we put on our calendar during our prime time.

I would suggest we put things we'd rather put on the back burner on our schedules during the hours we're at our best because some of the other items on our to-do lists are things we can do in our sleep that don't require our A-game. If you're not really a people person, or people easily annoy you, you may or may not want to set a meeting with them between 10:00 a.m. and 2:00 p.m. You just want to be strategic about your most productive hours and how you spend them. And depending on the structure of your family, that 4:00 p.m. to 10:00 p.m. is just as important, but not nearly as organized.

I realize some people are night owls and others are early risers. Only you can really know your prime time, but you want to make sure you have a strategy for it.

Hack 3: Say No

Saying no is hard.

To a boss.

To extended family.

To friends.

To birthday parties.

To weddings.

To social media.

To streaming services.

Sometimes it feels like we're not allowed to say no, as if we're prisoners to our communities' desires. I know any of the above can be deemed very important, but so is your mental health. Whose schedule is it? It's yours. You may not be able to say no to everyone and everything, but you can say no to someone or something. Start saying no where you can so you can produce the kind of margin your schedule needs for you to be the person you want to be.

Hack 4: Schedule Your Growth

When you say no to one area, you are inevitably saying yes to something you value more. Your growth and development should be one of those things.

One thing I think should be on all our calendars is learning. Learning can be as formal as auditing a class at your local community college, but you can also find ways to sneak informal learning in. Listening to podcasts on your commute is a great way to educate yourself. You might not have time to read a physical book, but do you have time to listen to one?

Studying your chosen industry and perfecting your craft is how you get better. Once we get out of school, some of us stop learning. That is not a way to go to the next level. You are going to find your skill set irrelevant and knowledge base outdated in an accelerated time frame. We all know the person who talks about their job like it's still 2005.

What is happening in your industry? In your neighborhood? Nationally? Globally? We should all schedule time to invest in our knowledge and growth. "The difference between where you are today and where you'll be five years from now will be found in the quality of books you've read," says entrepreneur and speaker Jim Rohn.[9] What reading do you need to put on your schedule over the next year?

Hack 5: Make Room for VIPs

We all need to make room for a few things on our calendar. We have to make time for the things we procrastinate on. We have to make time for learning and our own development. We also need to make time for the most important people in our lives.

Sometimes there is a lack of congruence in who gets our time and who matters the most to us. When you look at your calendar, in addition to where you spent the most time, *whom* did you spend the most time with? If we become the five people we spend the most time with, *who are you?*

Today I have a podcast recording session, a keynote, another podcast, and an NBA chapel service. That's a busy day, but I also have a lunch date with my wife. If you look at my calendar, I usually have two to three lunch dates with her a week. Someone else might wonder how I was going to make it work or even assume those lunches are the first thing to go when my schedule starts to get out of whack. Instead, the time I commit to family is what I protect the most. My schedule needs to reflect who I want to be: a committed husband and father.

Recently, I was offered a speaking gig that would have kept me in Chicago after an event I already had scheduled. It offered a lot of money—an amount I couldn't casually say no to. The only problem was it meant another night away from my family. Did I say no and regret the loss of extra income? Did I say yes and miss out on another Thursday with my wife and sons?

Here's what I did: I let my wife make the call. Sometimes making time for the people we love also means they get to give input into decisions about our time. When we share our lives with people, we don't get to run our schedules alone, nor should we want to.

"Most of us spend too much time on what is urgent, and not enough time on what is important," writes Stephen Covey.[10] You should value yourself and your loved ones more than the temptation to let the urgent or the loud organize your life for you.

One of the people you need to make time for is yourself. Your personal health, both mental and physical, should be a priority, and your schedule should reflect that. Which is why the next chapter is all about making time to rest.

CHAPTER RECAP

- We have no way of achieving our goals if we don't manage our time.
- If you don't value your time, other people definitely won't.
- Audit your calendar to find opportunities to trim time and to determine what you need to make time for.

- Put a date on your calendar that you're looking forward to.
- Schedule shorter meetings.
- Do your most important or dreaded tasks from 10:00 a.m. to 2:00 p.m.
- Say no to the extra stuff.
- Actively schedule your goals on your calendar.

DO THIS NOW

The Calendar Exercise

Welcome to your very own calendar audit. Pull out your calendar and look at the last month. By category, assess:

1. Where did you spend your time?
2. What was unnecessary (i.e., what can you stop doing)?
3. What do you wish you did more of (i.e., what can you start doing)?

CHAPTER 10

THE REST QUESTION

Do I have to do it all?

*I wanted to figure out why I was so busy, but
I couldn't find the time to do it.*
—Todd Stocker

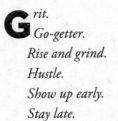rit.
Go-getter.
Rise and grind.
Hustle.
Show up early.
Stay late.

These are just a few of the words that encompass what most people believe their employers want from them. Then they add a splash of work-life balance.

Isn't it interesting that in the phrase "work-life balance" the word "work" always gets on the scale before "life"? Working to live can easily become living to work. As you can tell from this book, I like asking questions. One of the questions I ask often in my coaching practice is a very simple one: How are you?

The top responses I've received to that question in the 2020s are: tired, exhausted, and burnt out. Some people are legit physically tired. Others are emotionally exhausted from the media and politics. Others are psychologically burned out from carrying a heavy load and schedule that's not conducive for their long-term success.

What if words like *unplug, pace, pause,* and *sleep* were celebrated as much as the list of words at the top of this chapter? Ironically, most people say they want others to have work-life balance, but all of them still want an immediate response to their email, text, DM, and phone call. They fail to realize that in order to have work-life balance, others would have to say no—to *them*.

We're being asked to do and be more with less hours in the day. At the same time, the American workforce expectations remain high. The most dramatic change in the American workforce in the last century is the increasing participation of women. In 1950, 33.9 percent of women worked. That number was up to 43.3 percent in 1970, and 57 percent of women ages sixteen and older in the twenty-teens.[1]

Being a stay-at-home mom used to be the goal—or at least it was talked about that way. Traditional family rules were that Dad works and Mom changes diapers. If a mom had to work, that was notable. Notice we have the phrase "working moms," but no one says, "working dads."

The reality has always been more nuanced than the narrative. Black women have historically had a relatively high rate of employment, because staying at home was not an option. Way back in 1880, 35.4 percent of married Black women and 73.3 percent of single Black women worked versus 7.3 percent of married white women and 23.8 percent of single white women.[2] Now the numbers are more or less equal, but for a long time it was considered a success for Black women to stay home.

Now it's a little more complicated. Some women still feel pressured to stay home; others don't. At the same time, if *men* stay home, no one gives them their flowers. Being a stay-at-home dad can be seen as being shameful, like you can't provide for your family. But if both parents work, for both parents to have an equal opportunity, they have to redistribute all the household responsibilities equally. As any working parent knows, that can be really tough.

In the pandemic, for half of America, we all became stay-at-home parents. Then we became stay-at-home principals, stay-at-home English teachers, stay-at-home soccer coaches, and stay-at-home math tutors. I became a stay-at-home speaker and author. We were all wearing so many hats, which seemed impossible considering everything we were doing before. I don't know anyone who feels like they crushed it at everything they were expected to do and be.

Not to paint with broad strokes, but I think this gave us all a taste of what it was like for a lot of working moms even before the pandemic happened. Now all of us are expected to be everything to everybody, while also changing the world and being politically engaged and fit and having three cool hobbies.

This is the chapter where I tell you that, while this book is about growth, you cannot do it all. My intent is that you become a better person, not a perfect person. You also are a real human, and real humans need rest. They also need to value and care for themselves.

I will break down where some of the pressure to do it all comes from as well as actionable ways to build rest into your schedule. I understand that in the 2020s, with our demanding lives, making time for rest can feel impossible. But it is critical that we take care of ourselves and recharge.

RENAISSANCE HUMANS

There's this awesome phrase that we use to describe someone who can do tons of stuff well: a "Renaissance man" (or, in modern times, "human"). Do you know where this phrase came from? During the fifteenth and sixteenth centuries, the Renaissance—a time of innovation, intellectual exploration, and humanism following the Dark Ages—encouraged people—okay, mostly men—to acquire a diverse range of skills. Science, art, music, architecture—you name it, the Renaissance man had it covered. Think Leonardo da Vinci.

This was all well and good back in the 1400s when society (thankfully) looked *very* different—but how is it that, in the twenty-first century, we are *all* expected to be Renaissance humans?

In elementary school, we get trained in the idea that everything we do earns a grade. An A in spelling, a B- in typing, and a C in math. An 86 percent on your calculus test, or a 3.6 GPA. We are used to rating everything we do and, if we are high achievers, maxing out all our grades everywhere. It's the only way we're going to get into the right college or get our dream job.

That thinking carries into our adult lives. Now, instead of English, science, and math, we grade ourselves on all the different aspects of our lives—and there are a lot of them. Our lives exist in different categories, some overlapping but most competing. We are expected to do it all while getting a ten out of ten in every single part of our lives.

For most of us, the expectations we have of ourselves look like the following:

- Vocation: Be really good at your job. Excel in it. Get promoted. Earn bonuses. Climb the ladder. Make an impression. Take risks and look good while doing it. If you've been promoted in your life, that alone can make you feel like you're hitting 10 for 10 in this area. But if you're a leader, the expectations are far greater.
- Parenting: As parents, we are expected to knock it out of the park. We have to feed the kids well. Make sure they get good

grades. Be at every single event, even if we have multiple kids. If the events are at the same time, we should be at both. One of my friends has seven kids, and he needs to be in seven places at once. We need to be all in with *each* kid, not overall. You might feel like you're doing well with one child and failing completely with another. But who's creating the grading scale here?

- Marriage and Dating: In addition to all the administrative duties that modern relationships entail (keeping up a living space, managing finances, managing schedules, etc.), our marriages are also supposed to be loving, romantic, and affirming. We should simultaneously change diapers, do bath time and homework, and be romantic after a long day at work. Quality time with our spouses means that not only do we make dinner, but we also go on date nights. If we are dating, it's the same deal, but with the romance expectation dialed up to 11.

- Extended Family: Not only do we need to attend to our nuclear family, but we also need to make sure our parents, grandparents, siblings, aunts, uncles, nieces, nephews, cousins, and second cousins have relationships with us too. Attend their weddings, holiday celebrations, and backyard BBQs. We also need to send cards and buy graduation presents if we want the 10.

- Friendships: How many friends do you have on Facebook? The average person has 338.[3] Which means the average person has about twenty-seven days off a year where they don't have to remember somebody's birthday. That's 338 birthdays you need to remember, and people you need to be in communication with, at least by text, every year. (I'm exaggerating a little, but there's a real pressure to show up for our friends.) Birthdays, anniversaries, big life events—to be a 10 for 10 friend, we need to take care of all the above, as well as be in the loop on life events like illnesses, divorces, promotions, vacations, and new cars. With these expectations, it's likely we'll disappoint someone.

- Community Engagement: No longer is it enough to take care of our inner circles (family and friends); we now need to be engaged on a local, national, and even international level. Am I a good neighbor? Am I doing enough for my community? Am I involved at church? Am I aware of and informed about events happening on a global scale? To get 10 out of 10, I need to check all those boxes.

- Finances: We also need to be on top of our finances. Life in the United States is expensive. The cost of living increased by 6.7 percent in 2021 alone.[4] No longer can we leave it to the old give/save/spend model of sticking cash in savings accounts or under the mattress to ensure our housing and retirement through our golden years. Digital currency has changed the game, and now more than ever we need sophisticated personal financial skills to run our money—or we need to pay a lot of money to help someone manage it for us.

- Oh, and also . . . Health: We're expected to be healthy in mind, body, and soul. For people of faith, like myself, this creates even more expectations to take care of your soul. Emotionally stable, fit, and energized gets the 10 out of 10.

By the way, these expectations are assuming you've had no emergency of any kind. Because one little disruption can bring your scores down in any area.

What I'm gathering from my community is the expectation for all of us to:

- Excel in our careers. Look good. Read books. Listen to podcasts. Be awesome to other people.

- Raise healthy, triathlete children who get good grades and make smart decisions that make us look good when we show up to all of their events for fifteen years of their upbringing.
- Have thriving romantic relationships, consistently looking for the latest and greatest restaurants and vacation spots to prove it on social media.
- Be present with our family, friends, and colleagues while contributing to the world around us.
- And start off our days with yoga and a green smoothie, then cap off the day with a quinoa salad and a cool-down ride on our Peloton.

Am I missing anything on the list?

You might even have categories I haven't put on here, especially if you're taking online courses right now. But here's what I know: every single one of those categories requires one thing we already know is valuable—time.

Do you ever feel like you have those expectations, yet you don't know one other person who's successfully pulling it off? You might know someone who posts like they're accomplishing it, but do you actually know someone in real life who would score 10 out of 10 in all of those areas? (If you do, can you please email me their name and number, and I'll make sure HarperCollins gets them a book deal immediately.)

At some point we have to ask ourselves, Do I have to do it all? And where did the expectation to do it all come from?

The difficulty of hitting that 10 for 10 is compounded by various aspects of our identity and circumstances. For example, women have higher standards to hit in several areas of their lives. Mom guilt is real, as is the expectation that professional women look put together and attractive.

NOT GUILTY

In my experience ministering to and coaching people, I find that the perfectionist pressure to do it all starts externally and then becomes internal. Broadly, these pressures can be broken down into some mix of false standards, unfair expectations, guilt, and judgment.

The first idea we need to tackle and unpack is where we get our high standards from. I think in part they come from high-profile people who do a couple of those life categories well. For example, from what we gather on the internet, LeBron James is an all-time great basketball player, businessman, and family man. In the midst of his busy schedule, he finds time to sit courtside at his son's basketball game. And when he does, the sentiment is he's a good father.

Simultaneously, there's an expectation for parents to be at every extracurricular event their multiple kids have. But LeBron can't be at every game. Why? Because he has his own! I am sure he makes the games he can, but he is no less of a success as a father because he doesn't go to all his kids' games. I don't think LeBron does it all. I think LeBron does his best—and that's the standard I think we should all strive for.

Not only are celebrities—even the really nice ones—only making it work with lots of help, but I can guarantee that the mom or dad who you think is hitting tens has a lot more going on than you realize. If you had a front-row seat to their lives, you would understand that when you see high achievement, you are only getting the headlines.

You see that parent sitting across the soccer field with their perfect outfit and great car and think, *They really have it together.* It's like looking at someone's Instagram profile and believing it captures their whole life. Meanwhile, I am questioning if any of us really has it together.

Expectations and guilt go hand in hand. The burden of doing it all comes from the guilt of expecting yourself to crush all aspects of your life and then discovering you're human. Mom guilt. Dad guilt. Leader guilt. Brother guilt. Teacher guilt. Neighbor guilt. Soul guilt. If the expectation is to knock it out of the park every time, then we are all failing, and we all feel terrible about it.

This can happen in small but insidious ways. When I get home from a trip, I feel like I need to pay extra attention to my wife and kids, but my wife and kids need different things from me. My kids want me to get on the floor and play dinosaur. My wife wants to cuddle. These are two totally different modes to be in. Oddly, when I am doing one, I feel guilty about not doing the other. Then I remember a client I haven't reached out to lately, and I feel bad about that too. Guilt is a constant state of being because I'm constantly being pulled so many different directions.

Young parents often feel guilt when it comes to living up to a school's expectations. The kids are the ones getting grades on a particular subject, but for some reason the parents feel like they're getting graded on their parenting. Whether it is a parent-teacher conference or a track meet, the parent guilt is real. Every comment about their kid(s) either makes them feel extremely proud or extremely guilty.

Older parents I talk to often have guilt over their kids' decisions. The parents are in their forties, fifties, and sixties. The kids are in their teens, twenties, and thirties. They are all fully adults, but the bad decisions, career changes, unexpected pregnancies, and more feel like a reflection of how the parents guided their kids for eighteen years.

That guilt extends beyond the roles we are expected to fulfill to our achievements. Did we get into the best school? Get the best job? Get a promotion and a raise? No? Then we have achievement guilt. Even worse, guilt extends to our lack of care for ourselves. Did we eat a cheat meal without intending to? There's health guilt.

DON'T JUDGE ME

Guilt comes from unrealistic expectations on ourselves, but when we pass it around to one another, we move into judgment. We've even given it a name: guilt trips. It's a guilt journey that goes from me to you. We should be helping one another manage these wild expectations, but instead we keep imposing them, then passing judgment when others don't meet muster. I don't know the super-human who is getting all tens, but we are hard on one another about not being that person.

Part of parent guilt comes from how parents shame each other. When I go to soccer practice and my wife isn't with me, other parents notice. I know because they let me know. "Hey, where's your wife?" What I want to say is, "None of your business. She's at home living her life!" What I actually say is, "At home with our toddler," but I hear the unspoken judgment in their question: "What is so important that she is missing this practice?" Ma'am, it's practice. And we have more than the child you see here.

The judgment, expectations, unreasonable standards, and guilt can warp how we decide to live our lives. Any family can become kid-centric if the pressure to make it all about the kids takes root. Any person can become work-centric if they don't disentangle the pressure to achieve from what they really want.

The problem with crumbling under the expectations and guilt is that we lose sight of our goals while also resenting our lives. Something has to change.

936 SATURDAYS

At some point, that toxic mix of pressures became too much. Parental guilt was the first thing I decided needed to go. I got to a place where, when I am with my kids, I just want to enjoy them. I realized I had to change something when I counted the number of Saturdays I get with them before they turn eighteen. The answer was 936. Nine hundred thirty-six Saturdays before my kids go to college.

I saw that number and asked myself, "How many Saturdays do I want to spend speaking in or traveling to a church instead of being with my kids?" Because I speak in churches quite a bit, weekends add up real quick. But at the time of writing this book, I'm down to 564 Saturdays with my oldest before he goes to college. Those Saturdays go really fast. And I have to sit back and wonder if my schedule and ambitions are really helping me achieve my definition of success that very much includes spending more time with my family.

A lot of people believe if they aren't giving 110 percent all the time—if they take a break, take a vacation, don't take that 6:00 a.m. call, don't work every Saturday—they are going to fall behind. What has been applauded in the American workforce is getting up at 4:00 a.m. and working until midnight. No one gets a medal for leaving at 3:00 p.m. on a Thursday to go play some basketball with their kids.

I once heard someone say that sleep is for poor people, but I think it's for healthy people. You can be successful and rested. Some people think you have to choose between the two, but I don't think that's true. You know who else agrees? Bill Gates, Jack Ma, Jeff Bezos, Tim Cook, and Dolly Parton.[5] They all are on the record saying they need seven to eight hours to operate at their best.

Those people all got enough sleep and had plenty of success

waiting for them when their alarms went off. It is reassuring to know you can do both, but I would ask: How successful do we need to be? Sure, an upgraded life, gated communities, flying private, and five-star island vacations sounds amazing. But if you scaled back your goals and made a little more time for rest, would you be just as happy and successful with a little less?

DROP A BALL

Eventually, in the process of trying to juggle so many balls in the air, I got to a place where I realized an unsettling truth: you can drop a ball.

You're not a magician. I know you can drop a ball. The way I know this to be true is because you have already dropped them. You are not as good at juggling as you think you are, at least not for sustained periods of time. If I were you, instead of dropping balls unintentionally, I would pick and choose which I can afford to let fall. "Any vision of success has to admit what it's losing out on, where the element of loss is," says philosopher Alain de Botton.[6]

I am always keeping a lot of balls in the air. I am a husband, father, friend, brother, son, speaker, author, executive coach, chaplain, and podcaster holding on to the dream of getting a ten-day contract with an NBA team. Sometimes, I get caught in a bind and something on that list has to go. Something has to be last.

For me, it's my podcast. I like to give good energy to my podcast, but it is the last thing on my list of what I have to do to still be on track for my professional and personal goals. It is the thing I think about the least. It is the thing I can afford to lose. If I cut my podcast tomorrow, nothing about my impact, income, status, or life would really change. I get great interviews, but I hear, "Come on my podcast!" more than I hear, "I can't stop listening to yours."

The balls we choose to drop aren't just about work. My son's basketball season is about to start. It's very difficult for me to train with him and his friends while playing in a men's league myself. I can't do both, and something has to lose out. So, I choose his league over mine. While I'd love to tell my son I'll be at every game and every practice, it's just not true or realistic for my profession. What he is told is that Daddy will always do everything in his power to show up for him.

Some balls are about choosing what to pick up or drop daily. Maybe some days you don't make a beautiful homemade meal, even if you really like to cook. Maybe some days you make time for a great workout, while other days you just need a walk around the block. Maybe everything on your to-do list doesn't need to be done.

Other balls are seasonal. There are times we have more energy for our friendships and times when the most we can do is take care of our nuclear family. There are times when we are crushing it at work and times when we just need to get by. What we don't want to do is be reactively dropping balls we didn't mean to because we got overwhelmed. Some balls don't bounce back.

Brian Dyson, the CEO of Coca-Cola Enterprises, puts this perfectly: "Imagine life as a game in which you are juggling five balls in the air . . . work, family, health, friends, and spirit. . . . You will soon understand that work is a rubber ball. If you drop it, it will bounce back. But the other four balls—family, health, friends, and spirit—are made of glass. If you drop one of these, they will be irrevocably scuffed, marked, nicked, damaged, or even shattered."[7]

Your life might not fit neatly into one of those five categories, but the idea holds. Maybe "family" isn't one ball but seven. Some are rubber and some are glass. You need to be able to tell the difference so the thing you let go of isn't something with long-term impact that you may later regret.

When you begin assessing what it is you can let go of, start by putting everything on the table. When I sit with executives, they assume that everything they are doing is critical or they wouldn't have put it on their calendars to begin with. They tell me about some time- and soul-sucking activity that, to me, doesn't have a defensible impact.

"Don't do that anymore!" I tell them.

"What do you mean? Someone has to!"

But do they? What's going to happen if they don't?

Look at everything you are doing and ask yourself: worst-case scenario, what happens if this doesn't get done? Some things have no wiggle room, but others might be less mission critical than you think. This is taking the "What can I stop doing?" exercise from the scheduling chapter and leveling it up.

I take inspiration from lawyer, speaker, and bestselling author Bob Goff. Every Thursday, he quits something, whether it is having an office or letting go of a hurt. "Why?" people ask him when he lets them know he's resigning. "It's Thursday!" he tells them.[8]

The idea isn't to become unreliable or strip your life down to the nuts and bolts, but to make room for change and growth. "Eliminate some of the noise in your life and let your symphony have the stage again," Goff wrote to the Twitterverse.[9] We are all distractable and easily led into more commitments than we have time. What are you quitting this Thursday?

PROOF THE WORLD WILL KEEP MOVING WITHOUT US

By now, the answer to whether or not you have to do it all in order to be a better version of yourself should be clear. No one is doing it all, even the people who look like they are.

You might be able to pull off tens in all aspects of your life for a short period of time, but it isn't sustainable. Getting tens in all these arbitrary, impossible categories is not reflective of real success, which is measured against goals you thoughtfully designed and set for yourself.

Not only do I want you to remember to keep your focus on your goals, I also want to give you permission to be human. You're not perfect. You're just trying to take your personal and professional life to the next level without exhausting all of your resources to do it. Whatever ball you think you can't drop, you actually can.

Your motherhood, fatherhood, leadership, friendships, commitment to the company, and overall sanity aren't on the line with every decision. You can take a break and you will be okay. You can miss some stuff and you will be okay. I know it will all be okay because many of us had to miss a lot when we were required to quarantine for ten to fourteen days over the past couple of years and somehow the world kept spinning. (I had COVID-19 twice. I lost twenty days.) It's proof that the world kept moving without us.

During the pandemic, one of my favorite phrases I learned was "hard stop." This means I have no flexibility to extend our session past the scheduled time. I like to give people a heads-up at the beginning of a meeting that we have a hard stop. "I have a hard stop at one o'clock," I let them know. Occasionally, I even excuse myself from meetings when we hit five o'clock. "Y'all are doing great, but I have to get to dinner with my family." As long as I respectfully set the expectation beforehand, no one really minds.

I used to let people have more ownership of my time, especially if they were paying me, but now I set limits. My agents and clients know Ryan is a family man.

"Hey, can you stay for happy hour after the event and mingle?"

"I really, really want to, but I can't this time. Trying to be home for dinner. I will be there early and crush the event though, but if I don't put my kids to bed tonight, that's a loss for me personally in light of my definition of success."

If I don't set boundaries, I bleed time everywhere. Breaks are the first thing that go. I know that most people don't have that autonomy, but if you do, take advantage of it. Or, if you have that power over other people, give permission to them to enforce reasonable boundaries.

NO SERVICE

One year I was in Denver on a speaking engagement. I was there for a few days with some time off. *Where can I go to get a great view?* I thought, looking at the beautiful Rocky Mountains in the distance.

I got in my car and drove to the mountains. All of a sudden, I looked down at my phone and saw something I needed to see: No Service.

The words were so surprising, I felt like I had to sit with them for a second. "No service" meant that I couldn't be of service to anybody. Even when I fly, I get on the plane and immediately start trying to connect to the Wi-Fi. It felt so nice in that moment to be unreachable.

All of us have to ask: Where is our airplane mode? Where in our lives is there no service?

I was talking to the president of a financial institution recently about rest. "When are you taking vacation?" I asked him.

"I'm not," he said.

"What do you mean?"

"We just don't really do that around here."

I had to pause for a moment. I was curious. "What do you mean?"

"Well, we go to Mexico and stuff, but we bring our laptops."

Here's what the brilliant Maya Angelou has to say about that: "Every person needs to take one day away. A day in which one consciously separates the past from the future. Jobs, family, employers, and friends can exist one day without any one of us, and if our egos permit us to confess, they could exist eternally in our absence. Each person deserves a day away in which no problems are confronted, no solutions searched for. Each of us needs to withdraw from the cares which will not withdraw from us."[10]

Perhaps you've heard the phrase "money never sleeps." But money is made from cotton and linen! Neither of which need sleep. But people do.

The average McDonald's makes $2.7 million a year.[11] They are open seven days a week and many operate twenty-four hours a day.

The average Chick-fil-A makes $7 million a year—and they take off every Sunday, the busiest restaurant day of the week.[12]

There is value in rest. There is value in taking a break. You can accomplish more in six healthy days with one day off than seven exhausted working days with no break. You must trust that rest has value and that you have the ability to say no.

The president of that financial institution who doesn't take a vacation needs one. If you can't take a vacation, then you haven't built a great team. That guy was a great leader—but he needed to build a great team and then bring some of that balance back. The company would have been better for it.

From executives to interns, there will be different needs for rest. Some of us have done too much unplugging. We need to cancel our Netflix subscriptions and get back to the grind. But other people have been hitting it too hard. They should pause to watch a show or read a fiction book that has nothing to do with business! Maybe they even need a formal sabbatical.

We put unrealistic expectations on people, and then we all get caught in a cycle of trying to create an image of ourselves as being incredibly busy and successful. Ambition and achievement without direction look like success—but are they? We set these external markers of success and undervalue our need to rest. What is our definition of success? Is that marginal gain worth it? Where do we need to build in rest to make sure we can achieve not just our short-term but also our long-term goals?

CHAPTER RECAP

- We are all expected to be Renaissance humans—doing it all flawlessly in all aspects of our lives all the time.
- That expectation is reinforced by external and internal guilt, judgment, and shame.
- We need to learn that the world keeps moving without us—that we can drop a ball and it will all be okay.
- Figure out how to set boundaries around your time and when you need to switch into No Service mode.

DO THIS NOW

Write down all the things you think you have to do. Then prioritize the list by what you should give more of your attention to, and what you should potentially drop.

CHAPTER 11

THE FUN QUESTION

Am I enjoying it?

Don't take life too seriously! Nobody gets out alive anyway.
Smile. Be goofy. Take chances. Have fun. Inspire.
—Dawn Gluskin

Being successful is easy.

Okay, at least the blueprint for it sounds easy.

But the secrets to success aren't secrets. Thousands of authors have outlined what it takes to be successful. There's a mountain of data and research of the top 1 percent in the world and what their habits are. Do what they do, and you should get what they have. You've heard it all before.

Wake up early.

Read like crazy.

Listen to podcasts.

Take risks.

Put in your 10,000 hours to master your craft.

And voila! . . . you will be successful.

I think that's all mildly true. However, in the sea of tips and tricks to help us attain success, very little of it teaches us to enjoy it if we get it.

We can become so busy building, climbing, grinding, studying, presenting, posting, and grasping that we never get around to *enjoying*. The cultures of our homes and jobs can center around hard work so much that we never stop to enjoy them. We've yet to master the art of stopping and smelling the roses.

Just like we get handed a definition for success, we are also told what will make us happy. Depending on who we are and where we are born, our culture creates a definition of happy and works very hard to make us believe that if we achieve it, we'll be golden.

Sometimes, we believe money will make us happy. I saw a meme the other day that read: *Money can't buy you happiness, but it sure does make a nice down payment.* Money has its perks, but we've heard plenty of stories from extremely wealthy people that prove a luxury lifestyle does not equate to happiness.

It wasn't until I sat in rooms with multimillionaires that I learned money was no indicator of their happiness. I work with many clients who are upset their business grew by only 20 percent instead of 40 percent.

"We *failed*," they tell me in all seriousness.

"Did you?" I ask. "By whose standards?"

"Mine!"

Granted, I did tell them they should have their own definition of success, so I guess they had the right to feel like they failed. However, while they may not have accomplished all that they set out to do in a calendar year, they still had a lot of wins they could celebrate and enjoy. Have you ever gotten the thing you desperately wanted but simply failed to enjoy it?

I find it humorous the amount of people who live like failures and don't realize how successful they are. There's a lot of talk about the "1 percent" and the incredibly aspirational lifestyle they must have. What's interesting is that most people haven't stopped to consider whether or not they're in the top 1 percent. Did you know you can check?

There are websites that will tell you what your percentile is based on your age and income. If you are thirty-five and made $100,000 in the United States in 2020, you are in the 83rd percentile.[1] That's the top 17 percent in the country, which is the top 1 percent in the world for sure. In the US, you are not a one-percenter, but you are pretty close. Cross the $500,000 threshold, and you'll hit the elusive 1 percent.

Here is what I know about people who make six figures: they don't act like they're in the top 17 percent. They look to their left; they look to their right. They look at their neighbors. They look at their friends and strangers on the internet and see someone who has it better than they do. If they just had a little more—vacations, clothes, jewelry, cars, houses—they might be happy too. They spend more time thinking about what they don't have than enjoying what they do.

Does this envy drive people toward success? I don't think so. Are we just born unhappy? Again, I don't think so. Research suggests that we are all born with an innate "set level" of happiness. Some of us naturally enjoy life more than others, but further studies show that around 40 percent of our happiness is under our control.[2] Happiness, as it turns out, is more of a choice than a circumstance. It has little to do with our personalities or our income.

So little of our lives will be under our control, but how we feel about what happens is. Stephen R. Covey transcribes a favorite quote in one of his books: "Between stimulus and response lies a space. In that space lie our freedom and power to choose a response. In our response lies our growth and our happiness."[3]

Somewhere in the process of holding on to our life, liberty, and the pursuit of happiness, we may have allowed someone else to define happy for us.

Fortunately, the pursuit of happiness is not just for kindergartners, hippies, and Gen Zers. Did you know there is an actual science of happiness? We don't even need to create our own framework for happiness and enjoyment. All we have to do is fill in the blanks.

One of the foremost psychologists in America, Martin Seligman, the former president of the American Psychological Association (APA), made it his mission to study happiness. Psychology spent so much time on the disorders, he thought, why not apply the field positively to make everyone's life better?

Seligman spent years compiling and conducting research to learn what made people happy. He eventually came up with a theory that happiness has three dimensions: the pleasant life, the good life, and the meaningful life.[4]

The *pleasant life* is all about enjoyment—how we process our past, savor the present, and cultivate optimism about the future.

The *good life* is determined by our ability to embody six key virtues: wisdom and knowledge, courage, love and humanity, justice, temperance, and spirituality and transcendence.

The *meaningful life* is one with purpose.

Little did you know that, in previous chapters of this book, you were already learning to be not just a better but also a *happier* version of you. Coming up with your own definition of success (chapter 1) is your roadmap for a meaningful life. Asking how to be better (chapter 2) and how to live with integrity (chapter 8) will put you on the road to a good life. In this chapter, we will explore what it means to enjoy your life, i.e., the pleasant life.

Enjoying your success, celebrating the mundane, and being grateful for your life no matter the season are the foundations of a life well lived and well loved.

PERMISSION TO ENJOY YOUR SUCCESS

Of all the things that surprise me about my work, one of the strangest tasks I have is trying to help my clients and friends enjoy their success. I have watched a lot of wealthy people fail to enjoy the fruits of their labor. It would shock you how many well-compensated C-suite executives who seem to have it all—money, accolades, applause—have a very hard time getting up in the morning and enjoying it.

More of us than we think are in a position to spend our resources creating amazing experiences or adventures for ourselves. For some reason, we are resistant. One of my clients, who is very successful, was talking about how much he wanted to go to the Super Bowl, but he felt bad bailing on his office and team.

"Why don't you just take your entire team to the Super Bowl?" I asked.

"We can't do that!" he said. (Remember how I feel about "we don't do that here"?)

"You can't? Or you won't?" I replied.

"Won't" is fine, but at least admit that you are making a choice. There are so many people who could do crazy, fun things but they don't because they feel like they don't deserve it, or they believe it is irresponsible. Is this you? Maybe you need to save, but maybe you need to spend a little money and have some fun.

Fun for you may not be going to the Super Bowl, but I know people who say they wish they could go see their grandkids across the country more often. They have the ability to do so, but it's as if they are waiting for somebody's permission to book a flight. I have friends who make well into six figures who say they wish they could go see their favorite artist in concert, but never do. They can afford to do it, but it's like they're intimidated by Ticketmaster.

Yes, the tickets are probably expensive, but what isn't expensive? Houses are expensive. Furniture is expensive. I met a mom the other day who told me they spend $2,000 a month on sports between all of their kids' clubs, gear, and training costs. It's amazing what we will spare no expense on and where we get cheap. Just like your body needs rest, you also need to occasionally have a great time. Life is too short not to use your resources to enjoy it.

I respect financial planners who do more than try to maximize financial returns on their clients' assets. For example, one wealth manager I know interviews his clients to see what is important to them. If, for example, they love to travel, he makes sure a meaningful part of their budget is put in the travel bucket. If they are going to go on a trip, they should do it in the style they can afford and have an incredible time.

So many people hoard nice things and then refuse to enjoy them. There are people who buy cars that they never drive. "It's a collector's item," they say, but what's the point of having a car you never drive? You get a nice house, and then spend all your time worrying about it getting dirty. You keep it *pristine*. But what makes a house a home is life in the house—kids running through the hallways, people relaxing without reaching for a coaster. Do you want to live in a home or a museum?

I am guilty of this too. I don't collect cars or houses (I wish), but I am a sneakerhead. There are at least nine pairs of shoes in my closet that, if I died tomorrow, I would regret not having worn. That's right—there are shoes just sitting in boxes in my closet that I've never worn because wearing them would decrease their value. And at some point, I have to look at my own closet and wonder, *What's the point of having such valuable shoes if I never actually wear them?*

I had a moment of realization over the holidays. My father-in-law had bought a pair of low-top Jordan 11s that are pretty rare.

We were visiting him, and, in the middle of a Chicago blizzard, he went to take out the trash . . . in his new Jordans.

I flipped.

"Those are *not* take-out-the-trash shoes!" I told him.

He just looked at me. "Why get the shoes if you won't wear them?"

An excellent point. I'm still not wearing my best sneakers in the snow, but the sneakers should come out of the boxes at some point. I took inspiration from his example, and finally unboxed a pair of Retro Jordans and wore them to the gym.

"You're hooping in those?!" my friends asked.

I was! I decided I was going to enjoy the fact I have these shoes.

The point for you is this: we all need to stop and smell the roses, especially the roses we worked very hard to get.

25 FUN FREE THINGS TO DO IN DALLAS

With the text community I send encouraging messages to, one week this is what I wrote: "Hey! I give you full permission to enjoy your life this weekend. Go do something fun."

One guy immediately wrote back: "Everything fun costs money."

I sat with his text for a minute, and then sent him back a list I pulled from the internet, "25 Fun Free Things to Do in Dallas."[5]

Sometimes I think we can forget two of the most common pieces of conventional wisdom: first, money can't buy happiness, and second, the best things in life are free.

Not all of life can be highlights. If we *only* let ourselves have fun when we spend money, that might say more about us than it does about our bank accounts. "Only boring people get bored," wrote Charles Bukowski in *Hot Water Music*.[6] If you can only have fun in the VIP section at Coachella or ziplining in Hawaii or on the Jungle Cruise at Disneyland, you might be a boring person. Fun people don't get bored; curious people don't either.

Now, I'm not knocking vacations and parties. Those are experiences you can and should enjoy, especially if you worked hard for them (see above). Somewhere between the Super Bowl and twenty-five free things you can do in Dallas, you have to make space in your daily life for some fun. Whose consent do you need to enjoy your life or career?

Besides the obviously fun stuff, what *else* do we need to enjoy? It sounds crazy, but most people don't stop long enough to figure out what parts of their lives they actually like. We all can easily list what bothers us or what we would like to change. (Sometimes it's *who* bothers us and *who* we would like to change.) But what is on the list of things that make us happy? Are these all things that are expensive or rare?

We can get so caught up in getting through our days that we never stop and ask ourselves if we like any of what we are doing. Are you enjoying your job? I'm not asking if you have your *dream* job. Some people conflate the two, but they are totally different questions. Work is work, and even your dream job will have its challenges. Similarly, if the job you have now is a 24/7 grind, are you sure you are in the right line of work?

"I have looked in the mirror every morning and asked myself: 'If today were the last day of my life, would I want to do what I am about to do today?' And whenever the answer has been 'No' for too many days in a row, I know I need to change something," said, of all people, Steve Jobs in a Stanford University commencement speech.[7] You may need to cultivate gratitude for what you have, but you may also need to make changes. Life is too short to hate how you spend your time from 9:00 a.m. to 5:00 p.m.

Enjoyment isn't just about what you do but who is around you.

Are you enjoying *them*? Your family? Your friends? Your coworkers? Whom do you look forward to seeing? Who energizes you and makes you laugh? Whom do you dread? Who leaves you depleted of energy or feeling low? How much time are you spending with people who burn you out?

I saw a TED Talk some time ago by Gavin Pretor-Pinney called "Cloudy with a Chance of Joy."[8] Gavin is the founder of the Cloud Appreciation Society. The purpose of the Society is to promote nothing more than taking a moment to look at the sky. If anything, the pointlessness is the point. In an "eternally busy" digital world, Gavin believes more of us should find joy in activities as simple and free as watching clouds go by.

You don't have to become a cloud watcher, but you do need to know what there is to savor in your life. Either you need to build in more things, people, or activities you like, or you need to appreciate what you have. A helpful exercise is to take inventory of what you are grateful for. Write a list of activities, stuff, moments, people. We have the tendency not to realize something or someone's value until it is gone. There is an urgency to cherishing what we have now.

Developing an awareness of what we like about our lives can also help us put into perspective what we *don't* like. All the problems and drama we have been hyper-fixated on may not be the barriers to enjoyment we think they are.

LIFE IS DIFFICULT—ENJOY IT ANYWAY

Being unhappy is not difficult. Life is unpredictable, and we are all guaranteed some amount of hardship and loss. We also live in chaotic times (not that I need to remind anyone). Besides the tough stuff, we tend to be experts at how things could be better for us personally and professionally. We are the Dr. Phils of our own lives.

I see this tendency to overfocus on the negatives often in the workplace. It takes zero skills to complain about our jobs—our workload, our bosses, our coworkers, the hours, the pay. All that chatter around the watercooler or, now, on Slack. Many people think they've figured out all the problems. But identifying problems doesn't make you special; finding solutions does.

Think about how frustrating it is when your car breaks down. You have to get it towed, take it to the shop, figure out a loaner, and pay for expensive repairs. At best, it's an inconvenience and chore. At worst, it's a huge financial burden. But you have to actually *have* a car for this to be a problem. In many places in the world, owning a car is the utmost luxury. Only 17 percent of people in China and 6 percent in India own cars.[9] Maybe engine trouble isn't the worst problem to have.

I think about what it was like before the COVID-19 pandemic. We had no idea that someday in the future there would be a number of things we took for granted and would do anything to get back. No one in 2019 said, "I love being able to work without a mask." It is amazing, when your circumstances change, how grateful you are for what you lost.

We like to use events outside our control, like politics, to be mad. Every four years, half of the country is very upset at the outcome of our presidential election. Whether or not you enjoy the next four years is up to you, but I cannot hinge my happiness on who is president.

It isn't that I don't care or that I think politics aren't important. I am a voting citizen, and I respect people who are passionate about politics and policies. However, no politician will determine the trajectory of my joy. You can control my taxes but not my mood. We give people we don't even know way too much power over our emotional weather.

"We're so busy watching out for what's just ahead of us that we don't take time to enjoy where we are," said Bill Watterson, the famous artist behind the beloved comic strip *Calvin and Hobbes*.[10]

We all need to slow down enough to enjoy the seasons we have. We are always pushing happiness out into the future, making enjoyment contingent on some standard we set for ourselves. It's like we need permission to enjoy what we already have. We live with a lot of self-imposed limitations.

Our culture tries to build momentum into every part of our lives. When are we going to graduate? When are we going to buy a home? Is it our *forever* home? (That's a lot of expectation on brick and mortar.) Our society doesn't let people breathe.

If we have a startup, we are convinced we will be able to enjoy life when we raise money. Then, when are we going to raise again? Will the valuation be higher? When are we going to go public? What will the stock price be? Should the IPO have been priced better? How is the stock performing? What will the shareholders say? The bar is always going to be raised. Looking back, did we ever enjoy running our company? Or were we always too focused on the next thing?

I knew a woman who loved her home. It was her pride and joy, and she kept it pristine. Every day, her husband would drink his coffee, then take the empty cup and plop it on the counter. Just left it there. This habit drove her crazy. Not only was he being lazy, but he was messing with their perfect home. She couldn't stand it.

Later in life, the husband got a stomach ulcer that meant he could no longer drink coffee. Even though this meant no more abandoned mugs, the wife was not celebrating. "I would give anything to see that coffee cup again," she told me. The thing that used to infuriate her was now something she desperately missed.

Life is difficult. Enjoy it anyway. People are difficult. Enjoy them anyway. I know we might think we need to wait for ideal circumstances and people to come around before we can start enjoying them, but ideal isn't coming.

Every season has enough space in it for us to enjoy it. We need to enjoy our one-bedroom apartments. We need to enjoy our condos. If we live with our parents, we need to enjoy the free meal. Life doesn't have to be perfect for you to enjoy it. It doesn't even have to be good. Whatever season you are in, what can you be grateful for?

Someone called me the other day as I was walking through the Atlanta airport. "How are you?" he asked.

I thought about it for a moment. "I'm enjoying my life," I told him.

What an answer. I was traveling. I was tired. I was on my way to speak to five hundred sales reps from a medical device company. I love what I do, but I don't always love everything that goes along with it. Still, when I thought about it, *how lucky am I?*

I pride myself on being generous, but I was generous before I made a good living.

I love being happily married, but I also enjoyed the years I was single.

I love having kids, but I felt fulfilled before I was a father.

While I have celebrated every milestone, I didn't wait to be happy until I hit them.

Every age, every season, has something in it to enjoy. Most people wait for their circumstances to play out to decide how they're going to feel about their whole lives. "I'll be happy when . . ." or "I'll enjoy it when . . ." I live by the mantra: What if that day is never coming? What if *nothing ever changes*?

What if you never get married?

What if you never have kids?

What if you never make a fortune?

What if you have to live with chronic pain?

What if you become terminally ill?

We all need to embrace where we are. We don't know what we don't know. We don't know how long we get to enjoy the circumstances of our lives. People who aren't enjoying life need to look around and take stock of all the goodness. Even if you have been dealt a rough hand, you still get to decide if you are going to appreciate and enjoy life.

I don't want to diminish your circumstances, but I want to encourage you to enjoy your life. You might get the worst news, but there is no rule that endless sorrow always comes with pain. Pain and sadness are real; you can and should feel it. But you do not need to stay sad and depressed in order to weather the storm. Pain is in store for all of us. We all wear it differently.

A few years ago, I was in Chicago to shoot a segment for an interview. It was one of those terribly cold Chicago winter days. Most of the people on set were very grumpy, me included.

Not Bridgette. Bridgette was volunteering that day to help with filming. Bridgette was bald, and I couldn't tell if that was a fashion choice or a side effect. She was so positive, and I couldn't understand how she had so much joy. *Why is she so happy?* I kept wondering.

After about twenty minutes of her radiating sunshine, I had to ask. "What's your deal? How come you are so happy? Give me the scoop."

Her deal was that she had been diagnosed with a rare and inoperable brain tumor at the age of seven and an aggressive form of cancer three years prior to that day we were filming. She was twenty-one, and she had a life sentence. When she was first diagnosed, she had been told she had six months to live.

Since then she persisted, but it had not been easy. She'd had multiple seizures a week, had lupus, an aneurysm, three brain bleeds, and a stroke. She was wearing a medical boot at the time because of a fall down the stairs. On top of that, she had recently contracted COVID-19 and neither her taste nor smell had returned.

But somehow Bridgette enjoyed her life.

"Yeah, I could go tomorrow," she told me. Then she shrugged. Doctors had informed her she only had so much time left, so she needed to enjoy it. Her circumstances are far from ideal. She has everything nobody wants—and the one thing everyone needs. Bridgette was the happiest person I had ever met in my life.

"I made a decision that while cancer may define how I die, it would not define how I live," wrote Erwin Raphael McManus in the *The Last Arrow: Save Nothing for the Next Life*.[11]

We all have an expiration date. I read once that anything we are putting off for twenty years from now when we are less busy or have more time, we need to do now. Life is never going to slow down, and tomorrow is not guaranteed.

Enjoying life is an attitude. Whether you've been dealt a great hand or a bad one, are you enjoying the game? We are not playing poker; you can't fold and wait for the next round, a better hand. This is your one shot. Are you enjoying the fact you're here?

I give you permission to enjoy your life today.

CHAPTER RECAP

- Too often we let other people define happiness for us.
- A happy life has three scientifically proven components: the pleasant life, the good life, and the meaningful life.
- Enjoy the good things you have now, from your nice sneakers to the season you are in.
- Life is difficult. Enjoy it anyway. People are difficult. Enjoy them anyway.

DO THIS NOW

Count your blessings. Literally, write down the things that are good in your life and enjoy them. Write down the people you love, and enjoy them.

CHAPTER 12

THE TRANSPARENCY QUESTION

Who knows who I really am?

*The older I become the more I dream of a world
where I don't need so much armor.*
—J. M. Storm

Abercrombie & Fitch or FUBU?

Those were my options growing up as I was trying to figure out how to assimilate into a private school while still searching for acceptance in my own neighborhood. It's the psychology of conformity. It denotes the idea that we all become keenly aware of what behaviors are expected and rewarded in our circles in order to fit in.

Everyone feels the pressure to aim for a specific set of behaviors to get praise, high marks, and applause. In life, we're rewarded for certain actions and ways of being. Which is why, growing up, we all adhered to what was socially acceptable, even if it meant hiding our true selves to fit in.

As adults, we've further become products of our environments and our circles. Where does the circle think we should live? What car does the circle think we should drive? What does the circle consider fashionable? What does the circle think we should post? Here's a bigger one: What does the circle think we should believe?

It's amazing how much our circles dictate. Inevitably this leads us to a place where we begin calculating what it will cost us *not* to move with the herd. Will the circle reject us if we believe like, dress like, post like, vote like, spend like, or live like we actually want to? Can we really afford not to fit in? The more our decisions are swayed by external influences, the higher degree of inauthenticity we end up living with.

What happens when you attain the American dream, but can't really be yourself? You end up having what everyone else says is important, except when you get it, you realize you got it by being someone else.

Because what comes with conformity is not just learning the rewards for fitting in, but also learning the punishments for going out of bounds. What are the punishments for standing out for the all the wrong reasons? When you're in high school, you might not get asked to go to prom. When you're an adult, it could cost you your career.

The number of people I know who've been terminated from their jobs for a social media post is astounding. Therefore, we come to the conclusion that walking the company or party line is the highest form of actual social security. Being who other people want us to be gives us a false sense of acceptance while longing for the real thing.

You can't tell anyone you are having marriage problems.

You can't tell anyone your kids have fallen behind in school.

You can't tell anyone you are struggling with mental health.

You can't tell anyone you can't afford your medication.

You can't tell anyone you're in the middle of a court case.

You can't tell anyone you had to file for bankruptcy.

You can't tell anyone how you really feel about social issues.

Because then you'd be put in a category of people who are treated differently, rewarded differently, and, yes, punished differently.

What I've learned working with people all around the world is that I see a massive gap between their public lives and private lives.

Somewhere in their world, they got the message that it wasn't okay for them to be themselves. The larger the influence people have, the less they feel like they can keep it real.

NBA champion Draymond Green is known for speaking his mind despite the consequences of being fined numerous times by the NBA. He and Tom Brady were part of a conversation on HBO's *The Shop: Uninterrupted.*[1] On this episode, Tom Brady was asked if he ever had moments where he felt like pulling "a Draymond, maybe, and take the fine."

Tom Brady responded,

> What I say versus what I think are two totally different things. I would say 90 percent of what I say is probably not what I'm thinking. Which is a challenge, you know? I really admire people that can actually do that and say what they think because they invite a lot of other things into their life. And I think a part of me doesn't like conflict. So in the end, I just always try to play it super-flat.

You can win seven Super Bowls and have over $291 million in career earnings, but it still will not afford you the ability to fully be yourself.[2] Given the tension we've experienced over the past few years with race, I've often found myself playing peacemaker between Black friends and white friends. Neither side felt the space to really be themselves with the other. Black friends felt like their feelings wouldn't be validated if truly known. White friends didn't want to sound racist for asking a question. So, I'd end up with two friends on islands who just got better at being quiet.

That's what we all do when we fear the consequences of being our true selves. Sometimes people have received the message loud and clear from their employer that they should leave their problems at the door and just do their job. My company tries to help employers see how much more productive their employees would be if they didn't have to vacillate between two worlds every day.

Unfortunately, if you become too good at leaving your problems at the door, you will eventually become what you never sought out to be: a fraud.

Somewhere between who we really are on the inside, who we want to be in the future, and who we think we have to be to survive and be accepted, we just get lost. And if we don't know ourselves, how can anyone else know who we really are?

CODE-SWITCHING

Sometimes I think about all the groups of people who'd have something to lose if people knew who they really were. Every identity has expectations and limitations placed on them, performing a certain kind of masculinity, femininity, racial identity, or set of beliefs. The gap between our inner and outer selves shrinks and widens depending on the company we are in.

In the DEI fields, we call this "code-switching." We act certain ways based on who we are around. This is often a conversation among Black executives I work with. Who they are and how they talk at their jobs might sound completely different from how they talk at the barbershop. Hence, code-switching. When asked if they felt they could talk and act at work how they might talk and act at the gym with their friends—not a chance.

Being a motivational speaker, I'm consistently stepping into different industries. I have to be able to relate to everyone, from NBA All-Stars to factory workers to lawyers to health-care professionals to realtors to teachers to financial advisors to church audiences. What all those audiences have in common is that what they look for in a speaker is simple: a connection. Early in my career, I found myself code-switching more than I wanted to. Was I good at reading my audience, or was I pretending?

When I speak at events, sometimes I tell Walmart jokes and sometimes I tell Target jokes. If my Walmart peeps compared notes with my Target peeps, they might say, "I thought he shopped at our store." The truth is, I shop at both. The jokes I tell just depend on what city I'm in and what side of town I'm on. Remember, I grew up on two sides of town, so I speak both Walmart and Target fluently.

Have you ever code-switched? Have you ever had to change the way you talk or the way you act around a certain group in order to survive?

We face a few dangers code-switching as much as we do. The first is loneliness. You can be the most successful person in the world, where everyone knows your name—and nobody knows your pain.

A second danger is total implosion. What does that look like? Consider where people turn when they get to that dark place of secrecy, isolation, and loneliness. An alcohol or drug issue, gambling, the abuse of others. If you are angry and full of hurt, the world becomes your punching bag.

A third danger is that we further perpetuate the idea that other people can't be psychologically safe around us. Psychological safety is the belief that you won't be punished or humiliated for speaking up with ideas, questions, concerns, or mistakes. Do people feel that when they work with you? Do people feel that when they live with you?

FOUR WAYS TO START LIVING AUTHENTICALLY

Living a public life congruent with your private life does not happen overnight. In some cases, you might even need to fortify some walls to remain functional or safe. However, everyone can and should live more authentically than they do today. Here are four simple ways you can start bringing your real self into your home, your work, and your community.

Own Your Average

The problem with inauthenticity is that it is self-reinforcing. As soon as one person starts sharing only the best parts of his or her life, everyone else follows suit. It is infectious. How many times have you been part of a conversation where one person shared about a vacation, then you immediately began searching the archives of your mind to share a highlight of your own?

We get so caught up trying to live up to our image that we get further and further from who we are. "Everyone wants to be Cary Grant," said famed actor Cary Grant. "Even I want to be Cary Grant."[3]

The antidote to inauthenticity is simple: honesty. I learned this as I began to speak more honestly onstage. The more honest I am, the more honest the room becomes. The first person to be honest gives the entire room permission to do the same.

Whenever I share stories about my life online or offline, I have a choice to make. I can share highs or lows. I can share pains or gains. I can share moments where I received a standing ovation, or I can share stories of when I've been booed off the stage. (Okay, they've never actually booed out loud, but they've certainly displayed how underwhelmed they were by my presentation. I've had a few fall asleep.) However, what you get at the end of a year of ups and downs, highs and lows, joys and sorrows, positive and negative feedback . . . is average.

My friend Liz Bohannon has some excellent advice: own your average.[4] Her theory is that none of us is really as special as we would like to believe. I know we are all a couple of clicks and swipes away from seeing someone else whom we want to look like or be like, but in real life, the people you see on a daily basis aren't filtered or photoshopped. They're average. And what's wrong with that? I think we're so afraid of being average because we believe it'll make us less lovable, hirable, and followable.

But what if we just burst the bubble of persona? I have been doing this plenty lately. People will reach out all the time and tell me they want to write a book. I say, "Okay, are you prepared to write 75,000 words, only to have 45,000 of them actually printed?" I did three hours of research for one paragraph in this very book, and we eventually cut it. Seeing your name on a book at Barnes & Noble looks cool, but the process is actually grueling. Somewhere between the grind of writing a book and its being on a shelf in a retail store is an average existence.

People will reach out and say they'd like to travel and speak. Are you sure? Is your family sure? I consider it a privilege to be able to speak around the world, but that comes with a price my family and I pay. It also comes with very high expectations from clients. Over the course of one hundred-plus events a year, I take quite a few losses. It's not as glamorous as a social media post might make it seem.

The rise of Zoom unveiled our humanity. Kids run around in the background. Dogs bark. I Zoomed with a lady whose cats were in a full-on brawl in the background. It was rad. We've unintentionally invited people in to see the chaos that is actually our homes, and I think it's glorious. We have no choice but to show up a little more human and a little messier.

Do you know how many podcast recordings my son has interrupted in the last three years? Plenty! I used to pause and stop and have us start over or have the producer edit it out. But now . . . I say keep it! It's what happened in the conversation. I've learned that people admire perfection from a distance, but nobody can relate to it.

Remain Curious and Ask Questions

How many times has someone referenced a book, a story, a singer, a movie, or a show that you knew nothing about? Then, instead of just asking them, you nodded or laughed along. Why? Because we don't want to stand out for the wrong reasons.

I have been guilty of this many times. When I first got certified in the Enneagram, a personality-typing system, I was so afraid to say, "I don't know" whenever someone had a question about it that I didn't know how to answer. When I began preaching, people would ask me Bible questions and I never wanted to tell them, "I don't know" because I didn't want them to think less of me, but the truth is, I'm not all-knowing in any subject. But I didn't want people to know that.

Working with so many different industries, I've learned that every industry has their own language and acronyms. Have you ever been to a doctor, and they told you what was wrong with you in a language that made no sense to you? I remember my wife's doctor explaining what was happening to her body during pregnancy, and I had no earthly idea what was going on. I don't know who's in charge of naming medicines, prescriptions, or diseases, but I can't keep up.

I used to feel the pressure to nod my head and smile when I was confused because I was afraid of looking stupid. But what's worse is actually being ignorant and remaining that way because you're afraid to ask a question.

Recently, I was sitting in a meeting with executives from a restaurant chain and they kept talking about QSRs. "We want you to understand the culture of QSRs," they kept telling me.

Five years ago, I would have been like, "Of *course.*" Today, I like getting better and smarter.

"What's a QSR?" I asked.

They did what all my clients do when I ask a question: they laughed. "Yeah, why would you know that?" he said to me.

Why would *anyone* know that?

QSR stands for quick service restaurants. As opposed to an FSR, full-service restaurant, or an FCR, fast casual restaurant. It's what separates Panera and Chick-fil-A from McDonald's. I learned something new that day that I otherwise wouldn't have had I been too prideful to ask a question.

Do you know the number of meetings I've been in where I've asked what the acronym meant only for the person leading the meeting to discover that half the people in the room also had no idea? People are very, very afraid of looking dumb, even if it means they miss out on critical information.

There are some environments, personal and professional, that are hostile to questions. If you ask questions, you will be made to look dumb. I would counter that you are not dumb for asking the question; you would be dumb not to humble yourself and gain valuable intel! A real key in life is remaining curious and asking questions, even if you are afraid of what people might think of you.

Being willing to ask questions can transform a culture. No one needs to be the person who knows everything, but if you are willing to always learn and explore, you become a safe person to bring ideas to. You become a person others can call on, which is, arguably, better than being omnipotent.

Be Someone Else's Safe Space

This is a self-help book. Apparently, there are some rather unspoken rules I'm supposed to follow with this book being in that category. But if you haven't figured it out by now, I'm a Christian. There, I said it.

What's interesting is I've been told I shouldn't tell you that. I've been told that I shouldn't tell my clients that because it could cost me business. Because Christianity, in recent history, has become somewhat confusing. There are roughly over 45,000 Christian denominations globally.[5] Which means telling you I'm a Christian could lead you to wonder which kind of the 45,000 versions of Christianity I fit into.

I try to be one of those forgiving, love-your-enemy, generous, treat-others-how-I'd-like-to-be-treated, hard-working, make-space-for-other-people-who-aren't-like-me, and serve-amazing-grace-when-I-experience-flawed-human-beings-like-myself Christians. What makes me good at my job and my craft is anchored in the fact that I follow Jesus. When I show up at a church or a corporation, I'm going to do my very best to add value to the people in the audience, while being respectful of the values and mission of that organization.

But everyone needs to know, the smile they see on my face and the energy I bring to my work is a result of a relationship that I have with Jesus. I had one friend once tell me that a certain corporation won't hire people if they know they're a Christian. Well, then they won't hire me—because I am one. So what? I try to live my life in a way that makes space for other people to be themselves, while hoping they are doing the same for me.

I used to feel pressure to hide my faith. Have you ever felt pressure to hide who you really are?

I cannot guarantee that, as you begin living authentically, the world will be kind to you. However, if you fixate on how the world isn't safe enough for you or are upset that people can't handle the real you, this is time wasted worrying about circumstances outside your control. You can't control others, but you can decide how you are going to react when people step out and open themselves to you.

In your work environment, it is easy to point fingers at others as contributing to a toxic or overly political environment. Your leader might not be safe to be real with, but that doesn't mean you also have to be unsafe. Your organization may not be a safe place, but you can be a safe person. That is the core of what this book is about. Just because others can't rise to the occasion doesn't mean you have to stay at their level.

The more I have tried to be a safe place for others, the more they have returned the favor. The older I get, the more comfortable I become holding space for others. In my work, I have a front-row seat to people's lives. I sit with people from around the world, from so many sectors of life, longing to be themselves.

Everyone needs a safe space. A place to unload and be vulnerable is something most people don't have. Most people do not have a space to say, "I don't know what I'm doing." "I'm afraid for my kids." "I'm drowning in debt." "My marriage is falling apart." So many of us have no room to say our deepest secrets and fears out loud.

Who can you be that for? How are you going to react when your coworker cries? When your kid comes to you with a failure? When your parents can't cope anymore? Grace and nonjudgment is the best gift we can give others, even if we have to carefully navigate how much of ourselves we can show.

Everyone Does Not Have to Know, but Somebody Does

In both of my lines of work, ministry and corporate speaking, I have an ability to get people to tell me the truth. I can ask people small questions about themselves, creating space where, if they want to tell me about themselves, they are able to.

If you ask people about themselves long enough, they will tell you, especially if they know you are going to be equally honest about yourself. The more I made space for people to be authentic and vulnerable, the more I heard statements like:

"I've never told anyone this."

"You're the only one who knows."

"You're one of five people."

The irony of how much we are hiding is that most people have the same problems. We think we are unique, but our struggles are average too. It is mind-blowing how much pain we are all living with while putting up a happy front. Over and over, I hear:

"I'm struggling mentally."

"My marriage sucks."

"I'm burned out."

"I'm broke."

"I'm afraid."

"I don't know what I'm doing."

If one of these lands for you, you are not alone.

The mantra I want to encourage you with is this: everybody doesn't need to know who you really are, but somebody needs to know. You do not need to reveal your averageness or failures to everybody. There are some people who will take advantage of your honesty and treat you unkindly. Sometimes you encounter a person who is having a bad day and can't wait to have something they can use to drag you down to their level.

For the most part, though, the people we care about deserve our honesty. Selling a false image of our lives only creates distance. Then, when we need support, no one knows the truth of our lives.

I have spent so much time on PostSecret, a website and series of books started by Frank Warren. Warren put out an ad soliciting people's secrets. They would write an anonymous postcard and send it to him sharing something they had never told anyone else.

"My mother wrote all my papers in school, including my valedictorian speech."[6]

"When I told, my male friends were skeptical and wondered

what I had done to cause it. My female friends were disappointed that I hadn't reacted with appropriate strength and empowerment and courage. So, I stopped telling."

"It was silly. Now I am a lawyer, but my dad is still dead. All of this was for him. He never even saw it."

There was a range in severity, but reading Warren's first collection of secrets in his book changed my life. I had no idea the kinds of things people are carrying around. What are all of us hiding every day? What have we never told? What would we be so desperate to get off our chests that we would mail an anonymous postcard to a total stranger?

People with a mental illness don't want other people to know they are struggling. One friend compared his struggle with mental illness to being in a wave pool at a water park before they turn the waves on. He said, "It's like you're sitting there swimming with friends and a few of them have tubes they're lounging in, and then they turn on the waves and you're grasping for somebody else's tube, but nobody helps while you feel like you're drowning." Ever felt that way?

It is incredible the number of people struggling with anxiety, depression, and other disorders who have no room in their professional lives not to be okay. Even if their employer offers some form of psychological support, no one wants to take them up on it for fear of the consequences. One professional sports executive told me, "We spend millions of dollars a year on resources our players never utilize because they have a fear it will be used against them. And it could be." And that equally breaks my heart and fuels my passion to create safe spaces for athletes.

So many people are hiding relationship problems. They are crushing it at work, but things are not good at home. Did you ever have a coworker get divorced and you didn't know about it until the paperwork was already filed? You don't owe your coworkers an explanation of your life, but if you are having a hard time, do you really need to hide it?

Burnout is another serious issue people keep to themselves. Burnout is not telling your boss you are at your limit because you don't want him or her to think less of you. You are the teacher's pet, you are earning every promotion, and you are exhausted. Another statement I hear from leaders and people in positions of power is, "I don't know what I'm doing. If people find out, they won't trust or like me anymore."

Something else people tell me all the time is that they are waiting for some arbitrary future deadline to fix whatever is going on in their lives. "I'll put up with this until . . .

. . . I graduate."

. . . I get a promotion."

. . . I get out of debt."

. . . My equity vests."

. . . I get tenure."

Often that time horizon is about kids. "As soon as the kids are gone, I will . . ." That fill-in-the-blank could be a career change, a move, or even a divorce. I know parents who have a straight-up "Kids Countdown." They are waiting until 2026 to start living the life they want. See how silly that looks on paper? People never get around to fixing the thing that is actually broken. They choose to endure until that countdown is up, suffering the entire time with a smile plastered on their faces.

Once we lay out all these struggles that people are living with behind closed doors, it seems to me like we might be a bunch of liars. We are all trying to convince one another we are okay. We are all trying to convince one another our lives are ten times better than they are. Why are we pretending? What happens if we just let that go?

People hide because they have something to lose. We all have aspects of our identity that make us vulnerable. If we don't fit in with what we know others celebrate, we become afraid to be ourselves. The ultimate fear we have is: What are you going to do with the real me? If you knew this thing about me, how would you treat me?

The most liberating decision you can ever make is deciding to be you. I remember when I first decided, why not just be myself? Let's just see where the chips fall. That way, if people reject me, at least they're rejecting a real person. If I got celebrated, then it would be for the real me.

When you first start this journey, resist the urge to go ham. Public exposure is not the answer. Don't blog. Don't vlog. Don't whistleblow. Don't start a group text with fifty people.

I would love to tell people, "It's okay—you don't have to pretend anymore." But their bank accounts might say otherwise. The gap between who you are and who you have to be shouldn't be a gaping chasm, but we don't always get to be our full selves. Not everyone will treat us with dignity, and we should know that.

You don't need to share your vulnerabilities with the whole world, but *someone* has to know. Just one person. Maybe it's your spouse, your partner, your sister, or your friend. One person needs to know the truth of your life. What you find difficult. What you love. Whether you're enjoying it. One person needs to witness your triumphs and tragedies. Life is too difficult to go it alone.

Those secrets you are holding on to, about yourself or your actions, need another keeper. I'm not telling you to be a stronger person; I just want you to be more honest. I believe that God uses people despite their flaws. The sky is the limit for someone who is humble and honest. The people who lose themselves in the rat race and in their achievements are going to end up in a very lonely place. Authentic people have at least one person to count on as a friend and fan: themselves.

Slow down and take stock of your life. If you live without pretending, you will owe everyone else so little. Your conscience can be clear that you have served others well. You are able to step back and make space. You can slow down and ask, *Who knows who I really am? Am I proud of the person I show to others?*

This journey to acceptance and expression can take a long time, but you run the risk of paying a very high price if you do not attempt it.

"Being yourself is a continuous effort," writes James Clear. "There is always another expectation placed upon you, another person pulling you toward their preferences, another nudge from society to act a certain way. It's a daily battle to be yourself, not merely what the world wants you to be."[7]

You may not be able to be fully yourself everywhere, but you need to be able to be yourself somewhere. It would be a shame if you took your career and life to the next level but nobody actually knew the real you. Somebody needs to know who you really are.

CHAPTER RECAP

- Who we are becomes lost in the expectations people have of us.
- Own your average.
- Remain curious and ask questions. Be someone else's safe space.
- Not everyone has to know—but somebody does.

DO THIS NOW

Reveal just how human you are to one person.

CONCLUSION

Let's do a quick recap.

Do you know what it's like to be on the other side of you? It is better to err on the side of caution here and assume it could be better for everyone who experiences you.

Do you have *your* definition of success? Make sure it is yours and not someone else's. You don't want to wake up twenty years from now and realize you have fulfilled somebody else's dream.

How can you get better? Invite someone you trust to be honest with you and ask them to help you answer this one.

What credit can you give away? At least one person in your world is unnoticed and undervalued. Imagine what it would be like to find those people this week and give them credit. You might work next to them. You might sleep next to them.

What mistakes can you own? The words "I could be wrong" could be the difference between your keeping and losing relationships that matter the most. There could be someone you owe an apology to in your life or work. Remember, nobody wins in the blame game. You might own your mistakes and then wait for others to own theirs. But they may not be trying to level up. You are.

What risk do you need to take? You might have success doing things a certain way over a long period of time, but that's also a way to become bored and stagnant. Try something different. Be willing to fail and learn from it. Write a business plan for a new department. Go back to school. Ask her out on a date. Accept the fact that you were willing to try what most weren't. I've discovered that the more somebody continues to learn from their failures, the less they fail.

Whose dream can you support? It is easy to make your year all about your own goals. But what if you made it your goal to help somebody else go to the next level? Give them this book.

What's the right thing to do? I guarantee you will have the opportunity to cut a corner or cheat somebody in your world. Don't. It's not worth it. And you don't need to do it to win. The answer to this question can't always be proven, but it will always be felt. The people in your world should know you're trying to live with integrity.

How are you managing your time? Pick your favorite show from the last five years and look up how many hours and minutes it runs. This isn't to make you feel guilty, but it shows that you have time. You might spend the majority of your time putting out fires in your life and work. It can feel like there's always something going wrong. Take a deep breath and realize that you can control your schedule, or your schedule will control you.

Do you have to do it all? Shout-out to all the working moms. For every person who has felt the pressure to be great at everything, you don't have to. You can drop a ball because you already have. Just make sure you intentionally choose the right balls that can bounce back. You don't want to drop the ones that crack.

Are you enjoying life? If not, I give you permission to start today. Despite setbacks and challenges, you can still enjoy your life. Despite the difficult people you live and work with, you can still enjoy your relationships. Don't give your circumstances or another person that much power over your attitude about life.

Who knows who you really are? If you do the hard work of being yourself, don't go back. You may not be able to be yourself everywhere. You may not be able to be transparent with everyone, but you don't want to get to a point where many people know your name and no one knows your pain.

These are the questions that can help you go to the next level.

These are the questions that can help you become a next-level parent. A next-level spouse. A next-level partner. A next-level boss. A next-level employee. A next-level athlete. A next-level coach. A next-level teacher. A next-level lawyer. A next-level physician. A next-level influencer. A next-level entrepreneur. A next-level pastor. A next-level assistant. A next-level realtor. A next-level politician. A next-level neighbor. A next-level friend.

You may not be the CEO of your company, but you are the CEO of your own development. If you want to continue being encouraged to go to the next level, I send out an encouraging text to a community of people each week. To join that community, text "Leveling Up" to 469-809-1201. The next level is waiting for you.

ACKNOWLEDGMENTS

To my wife, thanks for playing a major role in helping me win at work and win at home. I couldn't do either without you.

To my children, thanks for grounding me in remembering what matters the most.

To my mother, thanks for being the only person on the planet who has prayed for me every day since I've been born.

To my oldest brother, thanks for always challenging the status quo.

To my middle brother, thanks for moving to Dallas, being a friend I didn't know I needed.

To Kelsey Grode, thanks for all your research and help putting this book together.

To Whitney Roman, thanks for playing quarterback at the Ryan Leak Group. There's no way I would have had time to write this book if you didn't carry what you do.

To Zach and Alex, thanks for always being down for an adventure and filming my rambles that sometimes turn into helpful content.

To Matt Sandberg, your craft is unparalleled. Thanks for taking what we do to the next level.

To my clients, thank you for letting my company add value to yours. Thank you for trusting me to make an impact on your leaders, teams, and employees.

To my church, thank you for giving me an opportunity to grow in my abilities to help other people take their faith to the next level.

NOTES

Introduction

1. Caroline Zaayer Kaufman, "How to Answer the Job Interview Question: 'What Do You Think of Your Previous Boss?'" Monster.com, accessed April 24, 2022, https://www.monster.com/career-advice/article/former-boss-job-interview?WT.mc_n=mktal_emp_rk_&ranMID=44607&ranEAID=2116208&ranSiteID=TnL5HPStwNw-JyRqkwE1gSJc.rvDqnj6iw.

Chapter 1: The Vision Question

1. Branford Shaw, "Top 10 Most Expensive Beanie Babies," Yahoo! November 26, 2021, https://www.yahoo.com/now/top-10-most-expensive-beanie-120059164.html.
2. Taylor Lorenz, "Young Creators Are Burning Out and Breaking Down," *New York Times*, June 8, 2021, https://www.nytimes.com/2021/06/08/style/creator-burnout-social-media.html.
3. "Gifted Men and Women Define Success Differently, 40-Year Study Says," Vanderbilt University, November 18, 2014, https://news.vanderbilt.edu/2014/11/18/gifted-men-and-women-define-success-differently-40-year-study-says/.
4. P. Brickman, D. Coates, R. Janoff-Bulman, "Lottery Winners and Accident Victims: Is Happiness Relative?" *Journal of Personality and Social Psychology* 36, no. 8 (August 1978): 917–27, https://doi.org/10.1037/0022–3514.36.8.917.
5. Soyoung Q. Park et al., "A Neural Link Between Generosity and Happiness," *Nature Communications* 8, July 11, 2017, https://www.nature.com/articles/ncomms15964.pdf?utm_medium=affiliate&utm_source=commission_junction&utm_campaign=3_nsn6445_deeplink_PID100085446&utm_content=deeplink.

Chapter 2: The Self-Awareness Question

1. "Biomythography," Cerritos College, accessed April 25, 2022, https://www.cerritos.edu/farbazaar/collectives_Biomythography.htm.
2. Merriam-Webster, s.v. "self-awareness (n.)," accessed April 25, 2022, https://www.merriam-webster.com/dictionary/self-awareness.
3. Tasha Eurich, "What Self-Awareness Really Is (and How to Cultivate It)," *Harvard Business Review*, January 4, 2018, https://hbr.org/2018/01/what-self-awareness-really-is-and-how-to-cultivate-it.
4. Kenneth Best, "Know Thyself: The Philosophy of Self-Knowledge," *UConn Today,* University of Connecticut, August 7, 2018, https://today.uconn.edu/2018/08/know-thyself-philosophy-self-knowledge/.
5. Tasha Eurich, "What Self-Awareness Really Is (and How to Cultivate It)," *Harvard Business Review*, January 4, 2018, https://hbr.org/2018/01/what-self-awareness-really-is-and-how-to-cultivate-it.
6. Tasha Eurich, "What Self-Awareness Really Is (and How to Cultivate It)," *Harvard Business Review*, January 4, 2018, https://hbr.org/2018/01/what-self-awareness-really-is-and-how-to-cultivate-it.

Chapter 3: The Self-Improvement Question

1. NBA.com Staff, "Legends Profile: Michael Jordan," NBA.com, September 14, 2021, https://www.nba.com/news/history-nba-legend-michael-jordan.
2. Levin, Marissa, "The 1 Thing You Need for Success, According to Michael Jordan and Tony Robbins," Inc.com, July 24, 2017, https://www.inc.com/marissa-levin/tony-robbins-and-michael-jordan-attribute-their-su.html
3. Ryan Holiday, Twitter post, December 5, 2021, https://twitter.com/RyanHoliday/status/1467524814768418816.
4. Bruce M. Anderson, "5 'Ridiculous' Ways Patagonia Has Built a Culture That Does Well and Does Good," September 27, 2019, https://www.linkedin.com/business/talent/blog/talent-connect/ways-patagonia-built-ridiculous-culture.
5. Cascade Team, "How Patagonia Became the Benchmark in Sustainable Clothing," August 20, 2021, https://www.cascade.app/strategy-factory/studies/patagonia-strategy-study.
6. Adam Grant, "How to Love Criticism," *WorkLife with Adam Grant*, podcast audio, March 2018, https://www.ted.com/talks/worklife_with_adam_grant_how_to_love_criticism/transcript.

Chapter 4: The Team Player Question

1. Damien Scott, "Cover Story Uncut: Drake Talks About Romance, Rap, and What's Really Real," *Complex*, November 15, 2011, https://www.complex.com/music/2011/11/cover-story-uncut-drake-talks-romance-rap-really-real.
2. "9 Scientists Who Didn't Get the Credit They Deserved," Oxford Royale, accessed April 25, 2022, https://www.oxford-royale.com/articles/9-scientists-didnt-get-credit-deserved/.
3. Marcia A. Nelson, "10 Famous Inventions that Come from Stolen Ideas," Thrive, January 14, 2019, https://thriveglobal.com/stories/10-famous-inventions-that-come-from-stolen-ideas/.
4. Nelson, "10 Famous Inventions that Come from Stolen Ideas."
5. Sharon Gaudin, "Facebook, ConnectU Reportedly Reach $65 Million Settlement," Computerworld, February 11, 2009. https://www.computerworld.com/article/2530833/facebook—connectu-reportedly-reach—65-million-settlement.html.
6. Gary Chapman, "Finding Hope for Your Desperate Marriage—Gary Chapman Part 2," Focus on the Family, March 27, 2019, YouTube video, 27:15, https://www.youtube.com/watch?v=cqoKkY-gnOk.
7. "Allen Iverson Crossover," NBA, March 22, 2007, YouTube video, 0:59, https://www.youtube.com/watch?v=zJMi5lvQqq8.
8. "Dean Berry (1995–1999)," HoyaBasketball.com, https://www.hoyabasketball.com/players/d_berry.htm.
9. Chris Palmer, "An Icon at 40: The Untold Story of Allen Iverson," BleacherReport.com, May 28, 2015, https://bleacherreport.com/articles/2476540-an-icon-at-40-the-untold-story-of-allen-iverson.

Chapter 5: The Humility Question

1. "You're Only Human (Second Wind)," by Billy Joel, disc 2, track 13 on Billy Joel, *Greatest Hits – Volume I & Volume II*, Columbia, 1985.
2. Clive Thompson, "Real Heroes Have the Guts to Admit They're Wrong," Wired.com, February 12, 2018, https://www.wired.com/story/real-heroes-have-the-guts-to-admit-theyre-wrong/.
3. Brian Resnick, "Intellectual Humility: The Importance of Knowing You Might Be Wrong," Vox, January 4, 2019, https://www.vox.com/science-and-health/2019/1/4/17989224/intellectual-humility-explained-psychology-replication.
4. Resnick, "Intellectual Humility."

5. "When Scientists Get It Wrong," *Science Friday*, audio podcast, June 11, 2021, https://www.sciencefriday.com/segments/when-scientists-get-it-wrong/.

6. Thompson, "Real Heroes Have the Guts to Admit They're Wrong."

Chapter 6: The Potential Question

1. "THE GAME OF LIFE Celebrates 50 Years," Hasbro, Inc., February 12, 2010, https://investor.hasbro.com/news-releases/news-release-details/game-life-celebrates-50-years.

2. Alicia H. Munnell, "The Average Retirement Age—An Update," Center for Retirement Research at Boston College, March 2015, https://crr.bc.edu/wp-content/uploads/2015/03/IB_15-4_508_rev.pdf.

3. Patrick Sisson, "Why Buying a House Today Is So Much Harder than in 1950," Curbed.com, April 10, 2018, https://archive.curbed.com/2018/4/10/17219786/buying-a-house-mortgage-government-gi-bill.

4. Lily Rothman, "Putting the Rising Cost of College in Perspective," *Time*, August 31, 2016, https://time.com/4472261/college-cost-history/.

5. Sharon E. Kirmeyer, PhD, and Brady E. Hamilton, PhD, "Childbearing Differences Among Three Generations of U.S. Women," NCHS Data Brief, no. 68, August 2011, https://www.cdc.gov/nchs/data/databriefs/db68.pdf.

6. Megan Leonhardt, "61% of Older Millennials Believe They'll Be Working at Least Part-Time During Retirement," CNBC, July 22, 2021, https://www.cnbc.com/2021/07/22/majority-of-older-millennials-believe-they-will-work-during-retirement.html.

7. Lyle Daly, "Average House Price by State 2021," The Ascent, August 5, 2021, https://www.fool.com/the-ascent/research/average-house-price-state/.

8. Melanie Hanson, "Average Cost of College & Tuition," Education Data Initiative, June 12, 2022, https://educationdata.org/average-cost-of-college.

9. Ashley Stahl, "New Study: Millennial Women Are Delaying Having Children Due to Their Careers," *Forbes*, May 1, 2020, https://www.forbes.com/sites/ashleystahl/2020/05/01/new-study-millennial-women-are-delaying-having-children-due-to-their-careers/?sh=84c8f13276ad.

10. "Supplemental Data Measuring the Effects of the Coronavirus (COVID-19) Pandemic on the Labor Market," Labor Force Statistics from the Current Population Survey, US Bureau of Labor Statistics, June 10, 2022, https://www.bls.gov/cps/effects-of-the-coronavirus-covid-19-pandemic.htm.

11. Carisa Parrish, MA, PhD, "How to Deal with Coronavirus Burnout and Pandemic Fatigue," Johns Hopkins Medicine, August 11, 2020, https://www.hopkinsmedicine.org/health/conditions-and-diseases/coronavirus/how-to-deal-with-coronavirus-burnout-and-pandemic-fatigue.; Aaron De Smet et al., "Overcoming Pandemic Fatigue: How to Reenergize Organizations for the Long Run," McKinsey & Company, November 25, 2020, https://www.mckinsey.com/business-functions/people-and-organizational-performance/our-insights/overcoming-pandemic-fatigue-how-to-reenergize-organizations-for-the-long-run.

12. Mark Murphy, "New Data Shows That Leaders Overestimate How Much Their Employees Want to Change," Forbes, February 19, 2016, https://www.forbes.com/sites/markmurphy/2016/02/19/new-data-shows-that-leaders-overestimate-how-much-their-employees-want-to-change/?sh=f149532162f6.

13. Britannica, s.v. "Heraclitus," https://www.britannica.com/biography/Heraclitus.

14. Sara Silver, "From the Filings: Supply Chain Lessons from the Pandemic," *Journal of Accountancy*, February 18, 2021, https://www.journalofaccountancy.com/news/2021/feb/supply-chain-lessons-from-coronavirus-pandemic.html.

15. @bobby, Twitter post, July 6, 2017, https://twitter.com/bobby/status/883046387780386817.

16. Karissa Giuliano, "19 Famous Companies that Originally Had Different Names," CNBC,

May 26, 2015, https://www.cnbc.com/2015/05/26/19-famous-companies-that-originally-had
-different-names.html.

17. Matt Seybold, "The Apocryphal Twain: 'The Things You Didn't Do,'" Center for Mark
Twain Studies, June 28, 2019, https://marktwainstudies.com/the-apocryphal-twain-the
-things-you-didnt-do/.

Chapter 7: The Assist Question

1. "ANDRE WALKER," AndreWalkerHair.com, https://andrewalkerhair.com/#andre-walker.

2. "Apple's Departing Chief Design Officer Was Steve Jobs' 'Right-Hand Man': Josh Lipton,"
Squawk Alley, CNBC, June 28, 2019, https://www.cnbc.com/video/2019/06/28/apples
-departing-chief-design-officer-was-steve-jobs-right-hand-man-josh-lipton.html.

3. David Hochman, "Jon Favreau on Speechwriting, Life After DC . . . and Melania Trump,"
New York Times, July 21, 2016, https://www.nytimes.com/2016/07/24/fashion/jon-favreau
-obama-speechwriter-melania-trump.html.

4. "Lis Lewis," thesingersworkshop.com, https://thesingersworkshop.com.

5. Dylan Dethier, "Why Tiger Woods' Ex-caddie Steve Williams Is the Star of the New HBO
Documentary," Golf.com, January 12, 2021, https://golf.com/news/steve-williams-caddie
-tiger-woods-documentary/; Jack Dougherty, "Who Has the Most Wins in PGA Tour
History?" Sportscasting.com, July 31, 2020, https://www.sportscasting.com/who-has-the
-most-wins-in-pga-tour-history/.

6. "Stephen Curry x Brandon Payne 2019: Efficiency, Reaction, Cover More Ground, Stay
Quicker Longer," LetsGoWarriors, YouTube video, 2:14, October 3, 2020, https://www
.youtube.com/watch?v=psVh1Ulecio.

7. "Chris Castaldi," IMDB, https://www.imdb.com/name/nm0005592/.

8. "Susan Batson," susanbatsonstudionyc.com, https://www.susanbatsonstudionyc.com/alumni.

9. Denise Petski, "High Noon Entertainment Ups Scott Feeley to President," Deadline.com,
April 26, 2018, https://deadline.com/2018/04/high-noon-entertainment-promoted-scott
-feeley-to-president-1202377093/.

10. Glenn Rowley, "Tina Knowles-Lawson Just Revealed Beyoncé Is Her Maiden Name,"
Billboard.com, September 16, 2020, https://www.billboard.com/music/pop/tina-knowles
-lawson-reveals-beyonce-is-her-maiden-name-9449802/.

11. Tuba Raqshan, "Like Father, Like Son," *Deccan Chronicle*, August 7, 2018, https://www
.deccanchronicle.com/150811/lifestyle-offbeat/article/father-son.

12. "Dr. Maya Angelou: 'Be a Rainbow in Somebody Else's Cloud,'" OWN, https://www.oprah
.com/own-digitaloriginals/dr-maya-angelou-try-to-be-a-rainbow-in-someone-elses-cloud
-video.

13. Dr. John Gottman, "How Can I Improve My Marriage in 30 Seconds?" YouTube video, 1:31,
The Gottman Institute, July 25, 2013, https://www.youtube.com/watch?v=G_Vz_Cbsu3o.

14. Mary Ann Stephens, "Becoming a Dream Detective," Marriage Insights, March 10, 2016,
https://marriageinsightsblog.wordpress.com/2016/03/10/becoming-a-dream-detective/.

15. Kathleen Elkins, "When a Competitor Tried to Buy Starbucks, Howard Schultz Was Rescued
by Bill Gates Sr.," Make It, CNBC, October 4, 2017, https://www.cnbc.com/2017/10/04/bill
-gates-sr-helped-howard-schultz-buy-starbucks.html.

16. @jimmydarts, TikTok account, https://www.tiktok.com/@jimmydarts.

17. @jimmydarts, Instagram post, December 13, 2021, https://www.instagram.com/p
/CXb9Ww3hnt3/.

18. @jimmydarts, TikTok post, https://www.tiktok.com/@jimmydarts/video/7072912704863849771?
is_from_webapp=1&sender_device=pc&web_id=7079417744219162154.

19. Justin Zackal, "Three Signs of a Miserable Job (and What You Can Do About It),"

HigherEdJobs, May 6, 2021, https://www.higheredjobs.com/Articles/articleDisplay.cfm?ID=2699.

20. Cameron DaSilva, "Andrew Whitworth Delivered One of the Best Speeches You'll Hear After Winning Walter Payton Man of the Year," RamsWire, February 10, 2022, https://theramswire.usatoday.com/2022/02/10/rams-andrew-whitworth-walter-payton-speech-video/.

21. Sonja Lyubomirsky, "Happiness for a Lifetime," *Greater Good Magazine*, University of California Berkeley, July 15, 2010, https://greatergood.berkeley.edu/article/item/happiness_for_a_lifetime.

Chapter 8: The Integrity Question

1. Paul Brian, "Infidelity Statistics (2021): How Much Cheating Is Going On?" HackSpirit, March 31, 2021, https://hackspirit.com/infidelity-statistics/.

2. "Anyone Who Doesn't Take Truth Seriously in Small Matters Cannot Be Trusted in Large Ones Either," QuoteInvestigator.com, https://quoteinvestigator.com/2014/04/15/large-truth/.

3. "Tax Cheating Statistics," EP Caine and Associates, https://cainecpa.com/tax-cheating-statistics/.

4. "Serena Williams: I Don't Need to Cheat to Win, 2018 US Open Press Conference," ESPN, YouTube video, 9:59, September 8, 2018, https://www.youtube.com/watch?v=bRa8kp_1zvI.

5. Reuters staff, "Blair in His Own Words," Reuters.com, May 10, 2007, https://www.reuters.com/article/us-britain-blair-quotes/blair-in-his-own-words-idUSL1037532920070510.

6. Stephen Miller, "Black Workers Still Earn Less Than Their White Counterparts," SHRM, June 11, 2020, https://www.shrm.org/resourcesandtools/hr-topics/compensation/pages/racial-wage-gaps-persistence-poses-challenge.aspx.

Chapter 9: The Schedule Question

1. Agence France-Presse, "Nearly 900,000 New Podcasts Launched Worldwide in 2020, Triple from the Year Before: Study," Gadgets360, February 4, 2021, https://gadgets360.com/entertainment/news/new-podcasts-2020–90000-chartable-study-research-spotify-2362865.

2. "YouTube by the Numbers: Stats, Demographics & Fun Facts," Omnicore, March 14, 2022, https://www.omnicoreagency.com/youtube-statistics/.

3. Darko Jacimovic, "Top Self-Help Industry Statistics," dealsonhealth, October 8, 2021, https://dealsonhealth.net/self-improvement-industry-statistics/.

4. "Insights on the E-Learning Global Market to 2026," Businesswire, September 27, 2021, https://www.businesswire.com/news/home/20210927005511/en/Insights-on-the-E-Learning-Global-Market-to-2026–by-Technology-Provider-Application-and-Region–ResearchAndMarkets.com.

5. Tony Robbins, *Awaken the Giant Within* (New York: Simon and Schuster, 2007), 25.

6. Gemma Curtis, "Your Life in Numbers," Dreams, April 28, 2021, https://www.dreams.co.uk/sleep-matters-club/your-life-in-numbers-infographic.

7. A. Pawlowski, "Monday Morning Is the Most Productive Time of the Week, Survey Finds," Today.com, August 20, 2021, https://www.today.com/health/monday-morning-most-productive-time-week-t228789; "Revealed: The Most Productive Time of the Day," Moneypenny, August 2021, https://www.moneypenny.com/us/resources/blog/revealed-the-most-productive-time-of-the-day/.

8. Melody Wilding, "Science Says These Are the Best Times to Learn and Create for Optimal Success," Inc.com, March 13, 2017, https://www.inc.com/melody-wilding/the-best-times-to-learn-and-create-according-to-science.html.

9. @successmagazine, Twitter post, *Success Magazine*, August 22, 2018, https://mobile.twitter.com/successmagazine/status/1032273856885608448.

10. Kevin Kruse, "Stephen Covey: 10 Quotes That Can Change Your Life," *Forbes*,

July 16, 2012, https://www.forbes.com/sites/kevinkruse/2012/07/16/the-7-habits
/?sh=724520639c6d.

Chapter 10: The Rest Question

1. "Women's Labor Force Participation," Institute for Women's Policy Research, accessed April 27, 2022, https://statusofwomendata.org/earnings-and-the-gender-wage-gap/womens -labor-force-participation/.
2. Nina Banks, "Black Women's Labor Market History Reveals Deep-Seated Race and Gender Discrimination," Economic Policy Institute, February 19, 2019, https://www.epi.org/blog /black-womens-labor-market-history-reveals-deep-seated-race-and-gender-discrimination/.
3. Kit Smith, "53 Incredible Facebook Statistics and Facts," Brandwatch, June 1, 2019, https:// www.brandwatch.com/blog/facebook-statistics/.
4. "Consumer Price Index—March 2022," Bureau of Labor Statistics, US Department of Labor, March 10, 2022, https://www.bls.gov/news.release/pdf/cpi.pdf.
5. Cory Stieg, "Bill Gates, Jeff Bezos and Other Highly Successful People Who Sleep 7 to 8 Hours a Night," Make It, CNBC, December 27, 2019, https://www.cnbc.com/2019/12/27 /how-many-hours-of-sleep-do-successful-people-get-each-night.html.
6. Alain de Botton, "A Kinder, Gentler Philosophy of Success," TED Talk, July 2009, https:// www.ted.com/talks/alain_de_botton_a_kinder_gentler_philosophy_of_success /transcript?language=en.
7. John Maxwell, "When a Ball Has to Drop, Make Sure It's the Right One," John C. Maxwell, June 17, 2014, https://www.johnmaxwell.com/blog/when-a-ball-has-to-drop-make-sure -its-the-right-one/.
8. "Quitting—Bob Goff," YouTube video, Resource Global, August 22, 2017, https://www .youtube.com/watch?v=85lDMQwKWn8.
9. @bobgoff, Twitter post, December 8, 2011, https://twitter.com/bobgoff/status /144779974405128192?lang=en.
10. Maya Angelou, *Wouldn't Take Nothing for My Journey Now* (New York: Random House, 1993).
11. Hayley Peterson, "Here's What It Costs to Open a McDonald's Restaurant," *Business Insider*, May 6, 2019, https://www.businessinsider.com/what-it-costs-to-open-a-mcdonalds-2014–11#.
12. Brittany De Lea, "This Is How Much the Average Chick-fil-A Made in 2020," FOX Business, July 26, 2021, https://www.foxbusiness.com/retail/how-much-average-chick-fil-a-made-2020.

Chapter 11: The Fun Question

1. PK, "Income Percentile Calculator for the United States," DQYDJ, accessed April 27, 2022, https://dqydj.com/income-percentile-calculator/.
2. Carolyn Gregoire, "This Is Scientific Proof Happiness Is A Choice," *Huffington Post*, December 6, 2017, https://www.huffpost.com/entry/scientific-proof-that-you_n_4384433.
3. Franz J. Vesely, PhD, Viktor Frankl Institute, https://www.univie.ac.at/logotherapy/quote _stimulus.html.
4. Martin Seligman, "Pursuit of Happiness," https://www.pursuit-of-happiness.org/history -of-happiness/martin-seligman-psychology/#:~:text=Seligman's%20conclusion%20is%20 that%20happiness,environment%20and%20our%20bodily%20needs.
5. Tanner Wilkes, "25 Fun Free Things to Do in Dallas, TX," Family Destinations Guide, February, 14, 2022, https://familydestinationsguide.com/free-things-to-do-in-dallas/.
6. Charles Bukowski, "White Dog Hunch," *Hot Water Music* (Santa Barbara: Black Sparrow Press, 2002).
7. "'You've Got to Find What You Love,' Jobs Says," Stanford University, June 14, 2005, https:// news.stanford.edu/2005/06/14/jobs-061505/.

8. Gavin Pretor-Pinney, "Cloudy with a Chance of Joy," TED Talk, June 2013, https://www.ted.com/talks/gavin_pretor_pinney_cloudy_with_a_chance_of_joy?language=en.

9. Jacob Poushter, "Car, Bike or Motorcycle? Depends on Where You Live," Pew Research Center, April 16, 2015, https://www.pewresearch.org/fact-tank/2015/04/16/car-bike-or-motorcycle-depends-on-where-you-live/.

10. Bill Watterson, *The Complete Calvin and Hobbes,* first printed in newspaper April 17, 1988, https://www.gocomics.com/calvinandhobbes/1988/04/17.

11. Erwin Raphael McManus, *The Last Arrow: Save Nothing for the Next Life* (Colorado Springs: Waterbrook, 2017).

Chapter 12: The Transparency Question

1. *The Shop: Uninterrupted*, Season 4, Episode 2, https://www.hbo.com/the-shop-uninterrupted/season-4/2-the-shop-uninterrupted.

2. John Duffley, "Tom Brady's Net Worth: How He Made a Boatload of Money During His Career," FanBuzz, February 1, 2022, https://fanbuzz.com/nfl/tom-brady-net-worth/.

3. Moira Macdonald, "Everybody Wants to Be Cary Grant. Even I Want to Be Cary Grant," *Seattle Times*, December 4, 2009, https://www.seattletimes.com/entertainment/movies/everybody-wants-to-be-cary-grant-even-i-want-to-be-cary-grant/.

4. Liz Bohannon, "Own Your Average," Global Leadership Network, October 17, 2019, https://globalleadership.org/articles/leading-yourself/own-your-average/.

5. Donavyn Coffey, "Why Does Christianity Have So Many Denominations?" LiveScience, February 27, 2021, https://www.livescience.com/christianity-denominations.html.

6. PostSecret, https://postsecret.com.

7. James Clear, "3–2–1: Being Yourself, Feeling Unqualified, and Win-Win Relationships," jamesclear.com, August 26, 2021, https://jamesclear.com/3-2-1/august-26-2021.

ABOUT THE AUTHOR

RYAN LEAK is an author, speaker, and executive coach who gets the opportunity to work with Fortune 500 companies, professional sports teams, and megachurches. Ryan speaks to over 50,000 people every month and trains over 20,000 leaders each year. He is the CEO of The Ryan Leak Group, an executive coaching practice that creates content and resources for leaders to take their careers and lives to the next level. He is known for his bestselling *book Chasing Failure* and for two documentaries: *The Surprise Wedding* and *Chasing Failure*. Ryan and his wife, Amanda, reside in Dallas, Texas, with their two children, Jaxson and Roman. For more information on Ryan, check out ryanleak.com.

THE RYAN LEAK GROUP

The Ryan Leak Group, LLC provides resources for people to take their lives and careers to the next level. To learn more about courses, workshops, keynotes, and coaching, go to ryanleak.com.